IMAGINED DIALOGUES

DIALOGUES

*Eastern European Literature
in Conversation
with American
and English Literature*

Gordana P. Crnković

Northwestern University Press
Evanston, Illinois

1004188568

Northwestern University Press
Evanston, Illinois 60208-4210

Copyright © 2000 by Northwestern University Press. Published 2000.
All rights reserved.

Printed in the United States of America

ISBN 0-8101-1717-7 (cloth)
ISBN 0-8101-1718-5 (paper)

Library of Congress Cataloging-in-Publication Data

Crnković, Gordana.
    Imagined dialogues : Eastern European literature in conversation with American and English
literature / Gordana P. Crnković.
        p.   cm. — (Rethinking theory)
    Includes bibliographical references and index.
    ISBN 0-8101-1717-7 — ISBN 0-8101-1718-5 (pbk.)
        1. Literature, Comparative—Slavic and American.   2. Literature, Comparative—American and
Slavic.   3. Literature, Comparative—Slavic and English.   4. Literature, Comparative—English
and Slavic.   I. Title: Eastern European literature in conversation with American and English
literature.   II. Title.   III. Series.

    PG502.5.C76   1999
    891.8—dc21   99-048789
                                                                                                          CIP

The paper used in this publication meets the minimum requirements of the American National
Standard for Information Sciences—Permanence of Paper for Printed Library Materials, ANSI
Z39.48—1984.

Imagined Dialogues

Rethinking Theory

GENERAL EDITOR

Gary Saul Morson

CONSULTING EDITORS

Robert Alter
Frederick Crews
John M. Ellis
Caryl Emerson

Contents

Acknowledgments

On both sides of the Atlantic, I have been very fortunate to work with people whose competence, rigor, and creativity provided an enduring inspiration for me and for this book. My warm gratitude goes to the University of Zagreb's comparative literature department, including Professors Zoran Kravar, Gordana Slabinac, and especially, Milivoj Solar, for his imagination and discipline in thinking about literature, and also to philosophy department professors Goran Švob, Neven Sesardić, the late Gajo Petrović, Milan Kangrga, Žarko Puhovski, and Nadežda Čačinović. Having been lucky enough to "land" at Stanford University when arriving in the United States, I pursued advanced studies in Stanford's Modern Thought and Literature Program, English and Slavic departments, with faculty members who have been unceasingly challenging and supportive as well as exceptionally open-minded in exploring different ways of relating to literature and helping me find my own way. Specifically, I would like to acknowledge Terry Castle, Herbert Lindenberger, and René Girard. The Stanford Humanities Center was always a welcoming place of interesting encounters and novel ideas; its former assistant director Charles Junkerman gracefully assisted me on many occasions.

My friends and colleagues at the University of Washington in Seattle helped me overcome the many difficulties large and small that arise from juggling the demands of teaching, writing, and raising a family. I am grateful for the expertise as well as good humor of Galya Diment, Katarzina Dziwirek, Sabrina Ramet, Karl Kramer, Jack Haney, Steven Shaviro, and Anthony Geist. Michael Biggins, head Slavic librarian at the University of Washington, is to be heartily thanked for his sure response to problems in locating certain resource materials. My students Yelena Furman, Christal Hawkins, Eric Kinzel, Brian Oles, Dana Sherry, Sofiya Yuzefpolskaya, and others have shared with me many hours of exciting discussions and have introduced fresh views that made me reconsider my own ideas.

Special gratitude is owed to Russell Berman of Stanford University's German and comparative literature departments, Marjorie Perloff of Stanford University's English department, and Andrew Wachtel of Northwestern University's Slavic department. It would take too much space to thank them individually for all they have done for me; I shall limit myself to saying that they accompanied this project from the very start and gave it much of their time and thought. They participated greatly in very different ways in the making of this book, and their generosity and steady support can hardly be appropriately acknowledged.

The manuscript itself has been significantly improved by suggestions from Gary Saul Morson of Northwestern University. As managing editor at Northwestern University Press, Sue Betz dealt carefully and perceptively with many issues that appeared in the course of the editing of the book. And it has been a special pleasure to work with Susan Harris, editor-in-chief of Northwestern University Press, and benefit firsthand from her dedication, judgment, and amiability.

Throughout the writing of the book my friends helped in many ways and provided cherished company and a healthy sense of perspective: Elizabeth Bohls, Katya Hokanson, Davorka Horvat, Davor Huić, Tin Ilakovac, Catalina Ilea, Sanja Klima, Peter Knutson, Hing Ng, Dunja Rogić, Vlasta and Bojan Turko, and Kamala Visweswaran.

Finally, I want to thank my family for their love, patience, and understanding.

Permissions

Emily Dickinson's poem "My Life had stood" reprinted by permission of the publishers and the trustees of Amherst College, from *The Poems of Emily Dickinson*, Thomas H. Johnson, ed. (Cambridge, Mass.: Belknap Press of Harvard University Press), copyright © 1951, 1955, 1979, 1983, by the president and fellows of Harvard College.

John Cage, brief excerpt from pages 96 and 97 of *Silence*, copyright © 1973, by John Cage, Wesleyan University Press, reprinted by permission of University Press of New England.

Gordana Crnković's article "Utopian America and the Language of Silence," a revised version of which appears in this volume, was originally published in *John Cage: Composed in America*, Marjorie Perloff and Charles Junkerman, eds. (Chicago: University of Chicago Press), copyright © 1994 by the University of Chicago. All rights reserved. Reprinted here by permission of the University of Chicago Press.

Gordana Crnković's article "That Other Place," a part of which appears in a revised form in this volume, was originally published in *Stanford Humanities Review* 1, nos. 2–3 (Fall/Winter, 1990): 133–40, and is reprinted by permission.

Gordana Crnković's article "Women Writers in Croatian and Serbian Literatures," a fraction of which appears in a revised form in this volume, was originally published in *Gender Politics in the Western Balkans*, Sabrina P. Ramet, ed., Pennsylvania State University Press, 1999, and is reprinted by permission.

Introduction

The Liberating Effect of Literature

A voice comes to one in the dark. Imagine.
—Samuel Beckett, *Company*

Something seems to have been forgotten in this age of murmurs about the increasing obsoleteness of literature in the face of electronic media, in this age of a dominant criticism which regards literature as only a part of wider discourses that construct various power relations, in this age of profound doubts among literary scholars about the subject of their study. What seems to have been forgotten is the primary reason which still makes many people pick up a good book, a reason found in the specific kind of joy expected from that encounter. I believe that my own experience of the reading of an inspiring literary work—an experience leading me to turn back to literature over and over again—is similar to that of many other people. It is simple and yet profound: something in us is smiling, even though the books' themes might not be pleasant at all; something is awoken, and something is born. The effect of reading a literary work is often that of liberation, even though we cannot quite tell from what we are being liberated.

And yet, while studying and teaching literature and literary criticism in both the former Yugoslavia and, during the last decade, in the United States, I kept seeing that many contemporary critical trends largely neglect or even flat out deny this liberating aspect of literature. I believe that this neglect has significantly weakened the study of literature, because it has alienated students and the wide readership that are attracted to literature precisely because of the unique and liberating response it provokes. People read literature because it has the potential to shed light on places that we were not aware even existed, to break through some spells that may have held us captive, to help us see and articulate our worlds and ourselves in new ways, to make us want to act differently, to reach out to our imagination as it envisions fuller lives and worlds—worlds that feel so much more familiar than the ones in which we may currently live.

I wrote *Imagined Dialogues* as an attempt to point out some of these liberating potentials of literature. The three chapters of this book are shaped as three dialogues between one Eastern European work, on one hand, and one American or English work, on the other. I have chosen works by the American John Cage (1912– 92), the Yugoslav Danilo Kiš (1935–89), the Pole Tadeusz Borowski (1922–51), the British Kazuo Ishiguro (born 1954), the Croatian Irena Vrkljan (born 1930), and the American Susan Howe (born 1937). Not expecting that the readers of this book would know all or any of the works I write about, I have provided a brief introduction to the works and their authors in each of the chapters.

The first of the three chapters constructs a dialogue on language between Danilo Kiš's stories on revolutionaries and Stalinist purges, *A Tomb for Boris Davidovich* (1976), and the collection of John Cage's avant-garde writings, *Silence* (1961); the second, a dialogue on power between Tadeusz Borowski's Auschwitz stories, *This Way for the Gas, Ladies and Gentlemen* (1948), and Kazuo Ishiguro's novel about an aging and supremely professional English butler, *The Remains of the Day* (1989); and the third, a dialogue on gender between Irena Vrkljan's autobiographical and experimental *Marina or About Biography* (1986) and Susan Howe's work that blends poetry and scholarship, *My Emily Dickinson* (1985). I decided to look at the realms of language, power, and gender—and at the ways in which these literary works help us achieve more liberated practices of language, power, and gender—because these three realms seem to be incessantly discussed in contemporary literary criticism, yet are mostly seen through the "eyes" of various theories rather than through the literary works themselves.

I shall talk more about this dialogical organization of the book, as well as about its main focus—revealing some liberating aspects of literature—in the second half of this introduction. At this point I would like to briefly outline the current critical tendencies which are neglectful of these liberating potentials of literature and to which my book, therefore, is an indirect response. Specific examples of these critical tendencies are taken mostly from the field of English and American literary studies; this is by far the biggest literary discipline, which to a greater or lesser extent sets the tone for all literary scholarship (including Slavic), especially in this era of the merging of different national literary departments. Needless to say, many original contemporary critics do not "follow" any of these trends but rather create idiosyncratic and highly inspiring work. Nevertheless, these critical tendencies or "schools" are omnipresent in the bulk of scholarship and teaching, because they can conveniently be turned into research methods that are easily taught to students as well as practiced by a host of scholars.

Putting Literature "Behind Bars" and a Few Problems of Historical Criticism

"Students nowadays seem to want to 'place' precisely, to locate precisely, everything about a writer's work: what he is, what has made him or her what they are, and so on," he [writer John Fowles] comments in an interview. "It seems to me that to imprison it is to deny something very essential about writing. . . . I feel this very strongly about writing and writers too. The world wants us caged, in one place, behind bars; it is very important we stay free."[1]

American academia in the last quarter century saw the rise of both historical and "political" readings of literature, which emphasized literature's connection with the "real world" around it, as well as literature's dealing with the issues of race, class, and gender, complemented with issues of sexuality, imperialism, postcolonialism, and so on. In the context of the mainly ahistorical (aside from literary history) and apolitical tradition of American literary scholarship, from New Criticism's close reading via Northrop Frye and Harold Bloom to Paul de Man and deconstruction, and in the context of Ronald Reagan and the immediate post-Reagan era, this trend was seen as radically oppositional by both its proponents and its critics. In opposition to previous scholarship which emphasized the aesthetic and specifically literary qualities, the historical and political readings pointed at the relation between literature and the various power dynamics and historical processes of the world around it.

Unlike previous American literary scholarship focusing on the specificity of literature and its "literariness" (to use the Russian Formalists' term), this newer criticism directly or indirectly promoted the concept of, as it were, the nonspecificity of literature, of literature's being the site of exactly the same social, cultural, and political processes which happen in the "real world," and which are identified and described by various social and cultural theories. Emphasizing the influence of social environment on the creation of literary works, critics have looked for the ways in which, say, the publishing industry, literary institutions, economic changes, or political processes affected literary production or were in turn affected by it (e.g., abolitionism in England as reflected in the works of Wordsworth and Coleridge). They also used sophisticated interpretative techniques to unearth traces of the specific historical and social processes in individual literary texts and to point out the ways in which these texts relate to such processes.

A cursory look at the catalogs of the academic publishing houses, featuring books just published or forthcoming, provides plenty of evidence for the strong presence of such historical literary scholarship. The language used in these catalogs rather boastfully underlines the difference between this new, historical approach to literature and previous nonhistorical studies. The American Gothic novel, for example, is "in this reappraisal" seen no longer as " 'escapist fiction' [of] ghosts [and] curses" but rather through "the complex historical circumstances that produced [that genre]" and as fiction "actively engaged with social, political and cultural concerns of the time."[2] Early (pre-seventeenth-century) English drama is now studied—"in contrast to the traditional emphasis"—"within the larger society" and its various "scrupulously reconstructed" contexts. The study of erotic literature of eighteenth-century France "argues for . . . an understanding of genre and of literary form as historical phenomena"; the early Victorian novel is seen through its interactions with "a set of texts generated by parliamentary and radical politics, the sanitation reform movement, and religion"; and nineteenth-century English Gothic fiction is studied with regard to the ways in which it was "used to shape a sense of English nationality during the century in which British imperial power was stretching out its greatest reach." The examples abound. Even though each one of these works seems like a fascinating, convincing, and inviting study, together they create a more uneasy effect of the hegemonic trend that has become the norm of the day, something quite akin to a critical and methodological dogma.

"Political" criticism, as I call it for the purpose of this introduction (and not using the term as synonymous with Marxist criticism the way some have used it), criticism concerned with issues that are commonly taken as political (gender, race, class, colonialism, and so on) and usually carried out in conjunction with historical research, has often been shaped in the form of New Historicism following the work of Michel Foucault. This criticism views literature as a part of broader discourses constructing gender, racial, colonial, and other relations of power. As such, literary works are seen as both reproducing and subverting these power discourses. Postcolonial criticism, for example, a trend inaugurated and shaped mainly by Edward Said's Foucault-inspired *Orientalism* (1979), primarily concerns itself with looking at how metropolitan literary works construct the colonial subject as inferior and in need of being ruled, thereby working hand in hand with the imperialist project.

One of the seminal articles in postcolonial studies, for instance, thus employs a precise language analysis of an eighteenth-century European travel journal (concerning a journey through southern Africa's land of the Bushmen) to display how European travel narratives commonly effaced the presence of indigenous people, as well as presented "newly discovered" lands in terms of "resources to be developed, landscapes to be peopled or repeopled by Europeans."[3] A recent postcolonial study of the Victorian era novels "demonstrates how images of domestic life can be incorporated into an ideology of imperial domination." On the other hand, postcolonial criticism also looks at the ways in which colonized nations employ their various forms of culture in the act of resisting imperialism. A new study of postcolonial drama (plays from widely different, but all formerly colonized regions such as Australia, Africa, Canada, and so forth), for example, shows how "performance has been instrumental in resisting the continual effects of imperialism" and how "post-colonial theatre can be seen as a reaction against colonial enterprises."

By seeing literature as part of the world's historical and political processes, and by researching the ways in which literature relates to these processes, both historical and political criticism shed light on previously unexplored territories. They have enlarged and enriched our critical appreciation of literature. Also, these kinds of criticism saw themselves as radically oppositional—and have indeed been oppositional—within the context of the American academy. However, despite their being genuinely enriching, useful, and oppositional, these types of criticism, at the same time, can be problematic and limiting in their own way. I would like to mention here a few problems of historical research, and the next section will discuss the shortcomings of political criticism.

First, I find it objectionable that historical research commonly presupposes that we know, before any contact with a specific literary work, what aspects constitute history and a specific historical context. We thus see our task as simply looking for the ways in which a literary work relates to one or another aspect of that context, such as, say, the parliamentary and radical politics or the sanitation reform movement of the early Victorian period. However, by assuming that we already know what a historical context is all about, we do not let the literary work create its own way of seeing and articulating this context, its own aspects and terms of history which we might not yet know and the awareness of which might be genuinely new. We do not let our own concepts of history be changed through the contact with literature, which, in this sense, can be "liberating."

Second, by being read through its imminent historical context, a literary work is reduced to this specific context, and it is not clear why, after all, this literary work (unless it is most contemporary and most local) should be of any concern to us here and now. Presuming that we are not particularly interested in the sanitation reform movement of early Victorian Britain, historical scholarship does not give us a good reason that we should be concerned with early Victorian fiction. Why is this fiction important for us today; what do we find in it?

Third, historical research tends to foster seeing a literary work as ultimately fully explainable by relations with its particular historical context. Literature is thus implicitly seen more as a product of interactions with its social and cultural context than as a result of the free agency of a writer and writing that can also go beyond this context. Diminishing the importance of the agency of an individual writer (or an individual literary work), on account of the overemphasized importance of a specific historical context, however, neglects the fact that literary practice does not relate only to its own space and time. As opposed to one's body, one's mind can travel freely and instantaneously. It relates to different historical periods, geographical spaces, imaginary realms, literary works, conceptual frames, numerous unretrievable elements of individual experience (the color of the sky on the morning a sentence was written, the expression on the face of a passerby, the sound of a bell), and many other aspects of one's intellectual universe, and it transforms them all, creating a new reality in the act of writing. If literary writing and the literary work are in some ways free (just as they are in some other ways constrained by their relations with their historical contexts but also by genre conventions, inherited poetical and aesthetic premises, and so on), then this freedom can hardly be explored by historical criticism.

I do not want to contest the rather self-evident fact that a literary text is an organic part of its historical context and is connected to this context in various ways. But I would argue that current literary scholarship puts too much emphasis on those connections and forgets that the freedom of a literary text is enacted within, but also—paradoxically—as an excess beyond, local historical givens. Historical research is interested mainly in this within, this "imprisoning" or "caging behind bars." I think that criticism should also look more at the paradoxical space of literary freedom beyond those bars. Such criticism should not go backward to the era before the advent of current historical scholarship but rather forward, forging an era in which we can ask—fully aware of the previous historical research—new questions about the freedom of literary works and about the things they do outside of their immediate historical contexts and concerns.

"You Never Know Where You Are with Production," or Literary Production at Odds with Political Values

They are, to put it bluntly, enemies of production. Production makes them uncomfortable. You never know where you are with production; production is the unforeseeable. You never know what's going to come out. And they themselves don't want to produce. They want to play the *apparatchik* and exercise control over other people. Every one of their criticisms contains a threat.[4] [Bertolt Brecht's characterization of the "socialist realism" critics who maintained that socialist literature had to be modeled on the realists of the nineteenth century, like Tolstoy and Balzac, and that it needed to avoid internal psychologization and formal experiments in order to "properly" show the totality of the world as explicated by Marx.]

A few years ago, I saw a very self-assured literature student roundly criticizing John Cage for not dealing with the issues of "race, class, and gender" in his work and also for not advancing more vehemently his homosexual orientation. This would not have been important as an isolated incident but is to me rather scary as an example of the attitude which seems to be fairly present both in and outside the academy, in mainstream literary criticism. Such political criticism, as I call it for the purposes of this introduction, often takes for granted that there is a fairly fixed set of progressive ideas of what the world is about (class conflict, racial oppression, patriarchy, homophobia, and so on), and consequently of what is "good" and "bad" in literature and the other arts.

To put it in a simplified way, this criticism maintains that it is good if literature focuses on and deals with the world's major problems, and it is bad not to do so. Good literature indirectly expounds progressive ways of seeing the world by making us aware of the dominant social (and thus also cultural, political, and existential) problems. Bad literature promotes conservative ideas or is altogether indifferent to "political" issues. Thus, good writers, such as this "century's two greatest American novelists" (as Faulkner and Morrison are called in one catalog description), "contribute to America's struggle with race," and classical American literature ("from Emerson and Poe, to Henry James and Chopin") is seen as mainly related "to the two great political movements of the nineteenth century: the abolition of slavery and the women's rights movement."[5]

The problem of political criticism does not lie in its individual tenets of belief; patriarchy, racism, and homophobia doubtlessly affect our worlds gravely, victimize people, and need to be overcome. The problem, in the words of the Polish writer Witold Gombrowicz, is not in the ideas but in "man's attitude toward the idea," an attitude that allows a person "to be duped by his own words of wisdom."[6] "[T]here is nothing simpler than to have healthy ideals, but it is hard not to falsify minute details in the name of great ideals."[7] The problem of political literary criticism is that it falsifies the "details" of literature—the multitude of ways in which literature functions and relates to its readers—by regarding literature as ultimately not much more than a didactic vehicle of established ways of seeing the world.

Lost in such criticism is the notion that a literary work (or indeed any artistic work) does not only relate—or not—to known political values but also creates its own set of notions about what the world is, its own specific view of the world, its own new terms of seeing the world, of "good" and "bad," of limiting and liberating. Instead of activating the potential of literature to actually say something new, this criticism simply applies the already existent concepts to the text. We do not look at what John Cage's work does; instead, we check his work against a finite list of values and pass the verdict accordingly. And the ideas that are progressive in the context of a conservative society and ongoing social struggles become unambiguously repressive—and start to "contain a threat"—when applied in such a way to literary works, asking for allegiance, denouncing true "otherness," and setting the only possible terms of acceptable practice.[8]

Literary works have the ability of making realms different from the ones we live in, realms that by themselves—by their uniqueness and freedom—indirectly but forcefully make things like chauvinism or homophobia or, for that matter, dogmatic literary criticism, feel unpalatable. Despite allegations telling us that we must feel otherwise on account of some works' political "indifference" or "impropriety," we should respect our own response to a literary work, a response affirming that there is something genuinely alive and liberating in these works, something to which we respond by becoming more alive and alert ourselves, and something that operates in a space different from that of recognizable political values.

"You Poor Thing, Then You Are Lost!": The Supremacy of Theory over Literary Criticism and Literature

Sometime in the 1920s, when a young Italian philosophy student named Ernesto Grassi paid a visit in Freiburg to the renowned older philosopher Edmund Husserl, Husserl told him that Grassi had good chances of becoming a genuine philosopher. Being an Italian, Husserl reasoned, Grassi was not burdened with the history of philosophy the way Germans were and could consequently attempt to approach the phenomena more directly. Dismayed, Grassi replied that this was not the case. Indeed, he went on to explain, he was actually very aware of the history of philosophy and had been educated on Hegel. A shocked Husserl then exclaimed: "You poor thing, then you are lost! Then you do not have the possibility to philosophize any more."[9]

Like many of my fellow students at the University of Zagreb in the early 1980s, I had been pursuing two majors—comparative literature and philosophy—for five long years, enjoying the pains and pleasures of the tension between the two. It was then and afterward, during graduate studies at Stanford University's program "Modern Thought and Literature" and later on in my work, that I found out that philosophy could be both freeing and limiting, depending on my attitude toward it. On the one hand, it could show me many ways in which my perception and thinking were grounded in basic premises of which I was never aware, make me see the world in completely different ways, as well as help me become aware of previously unperceived aspects of this world. On the other hand, it could also be limiting and imprisoning, when it cast such a strong conceptual net over things that I could not see them except in the ways grasped from my readings. This was when I wished I had read less of Hegel or Wittgenstein because I felt captive to their thinking and wanted—after going through it the best I could—to get out of it. Or, rather, I wanted to be both inside and outside of philosophy, to relate to it freely but not be subjugated to it, to take it in the terms in which it was meant to be taken—helping the reader to achieve some independence of mind, not making him or her a subject of this or that philosophy turned into ideology.

My personal situation described above—being sometimes restrained rather than emancipated by various philosophies—bears some resemblance to the current state of literary scholarship in the United States, specifically to the supremacy of literary theory in literary scholarship and, ultimately, the dominance of theory over literature itself. Given the current reign of literary theory, a scholar rarely writes without at least some reference to a prominent theorist or philosopher like

Derrida, Foucault, Baudrillard, Barthes, Deleuze and Guattari, Kristeva, Irigaray, Freud, Benjamin, Adorno, and others. Of course, the problem is not that literary scholars respond to theory or become more aware of the basic theoretical premises of their own critical work, but the fact that theory is often turned into a premade conceptual framework through which one views literature.

Theory used as a methodology, in other words, has gained supremacy over literature. The language of the academic publishing house catalogs seems to emphasize this supremacy. For instance, "*drawing* on feminist criticism, cultural studies, and the new historicism, the author surveys eighteenth-century literary texts" (italics mine). Another author is described as "*drawing* on the work of Michel Foucault and other theoreticians" (italics mine); yet another's work is characterized "as an explicit development of Foucault's work." "The great virtue" of the scholarly book is in "its ability to synthesize a range of theoretical ideas—whether formalist, structuralist, or 'reader-response.' " The practice whereby "critical theories are transformed into literary criticism and methodology" and "theory becomes literary criticism" is an acknowledged and valued fact of scholarship. Whereas one of the traditional goals of philosophy is intellectual maturity—to have the courage to think for yourself—literary scholarship nowadays too often uses various theories in exactly the opposite way, like doctrines that tell what literature is about by providing a blueprint for reading it. Concepts such as language, power, and gender have become oversaturated with their theoretical constructions. These concepts are now constituted with regard to a constellation of theories that are literary not because they are derived from literature, but because they are applied to literature. Potent theories (the provenance of, for example, Marx, Freud, or Nietzsche, or of the more contemporary Derrida, Lacan, or Foucault) are applied to literary works in the sense that literature is read through concepts and terms provided by those theories, terms such as the "mirror-stage," the "endless displacement of meaning and deconstruction of binary opposites," and "the colonial power discourses."[10]

The same problem occurs as with historical and political readings—instead of culling our insights and concepts from literature, we get them from our various theories and then simply apply them to literature. Literature's potentials to get outside of the scope of the existent theories, to make its own distinct "knowledge," are neglected.

The critical tendencies outlined above preclude, to an extent, the appreciation of both the specificity of literature and its liberating potentials. Historical research brings literature to the level of its local historical context and can speak of literature mostly in terms already established for this historical context. Through a more or less sophisticated reading of political issues, literature is brought to the level of these issues. By using literary theories as frames through which we see literature, a literary work is brought to the level of already existent theoretical concepts, without the ability to say something radically different and new.

Together these three tendencies cause a certain loss of what makes literature unique and different from other types of cultural production. Leveled with a sociohistorical context, political issues, or prominent theoretical categories, the uniqueness of literature is overshadowed. Dominant in contemporary critical work, these three tendencies do not address the fundamental question: why do we, after all, read literature?

The Other Way Around: Literature's Own Articulation of "Closures" and Liberating Practices

In this book, I have attempted to show some of the genuinely liberating potentials of literature that are not addressed sufficiently in currently prominent critical trends. My focus is not on the pregiven concepts of oppositionality and subversion, on what is established as political, but rather on what literary works themselves articulate as limiting and liberating. Tracing the feeling of emancipation in contact with a literary work, this book tries to answer two main questions: where does this emancipation stem from; and what does it emancipate the reader from?

Before and outside of the contact with a literary work, we—the readers—might not be aware of something that limits us. We learn about this limiting "something" through the liberating chemistry of our encounter with a literary work, where we might try to grasp the nature of that liberation. What was it we were liberated from? How did it happen? Through its liberating effects, a literary work at the same time indirectly points at that which it liberates us from. A simple example of this can be a situation in which imagination and playfulness present in a literary work can help us activate our own hidden potentials for being imaginative and playful. By so doing, they might also make us more aware of the prosaic, mechanistic, and repetitive frames that govern our lives. In other words, a literary work provokes a liberating reaction (e.g., a reader's playfulness), which, in turn, points at something (the lack of playfulness in everyday life) that is now articulated as a limitation precisely by and through this opposing and liberating literary reaction, and not before and outside of it, independent of the act of reading. It is precisely when we experience playfulness in our contact with a literary work, that we can feel the lack of it in our everyday lives.

In my book, I use the term "closure" when referring to the various limitations that literature articulates by reacting to them. My notion of "closure" stands for a broad variety of conceptual and social frames that "enclose" people within a given mode of life and prevent the breakthrough of new and liberating ways of thinking and acting.[11]

The three chapters of this book focus on closures regarding language, power, and gender. As I mentioned earlier, I have chosen these three realms because they have been incessantly defined and overdefined in recent theoretical work. When talking about language, power, and gender, literary scholars have customarily looked at literary texts through the eyes of, say, Derrida (language), Foucault (power), various feminist theories (gender), or some combination of the above. But what happens if we try to see those realms, their limiting and liberating potentials, their closures and breakthroughs, not through the eyes of theories but through the eyes of the literary works themselves? Instead of applying theory onto literature, can we not learn about language, power, and gender from literature?

In trying to do this, we do not have to somehow erase our accumulated philosophical and theoretical knowledge, our studies of numerous inspiring "non-literary" texts that have, together with other things, informed and changed our reading capacities and become the inextricable parts of the very texture of our minds. However, we should stay alert not to simply apply theoretical concepts onto literature and search for a realization of the phenomenon already conceptualized outside of literature, whereby existing theories necessarily gain the primacy of a dominant text. Instead, we can allow literature to say something substantially new and change our preexisting ideas, and to be the originator of new insights that are both more elastic and complex than any theory turned into positive knowledge can be and that tell new things both about the closures which constrain us and the practices which can set us free. As John Cage puts it, "there is at least the possibility of looking anywhere, not just where someone arranged you should."[12]

Connectedness and Dialogue

As a young writer, in Prague, I detested the word "generation," whose smell of the herd put me off. The first time I had the sense of being connected to others was later, in France, reading *Terra Nostra* by Carlos Fuentes. How was it possible that someone from another continent, so distant from me in itinerary and background, should be possessed by the same . . . obsession that till then I had naïvely considered to be mine alone?[13]

Based on the principle that nation is the main criterion of the categorization of literary works, literary scholarship shaped within national disciplines encloses literary works within their national contexts. The "field of action" of a literary work is thus mainly limited to its national context, and it is not seen how this work can relate to other places. By and large, literature is still seen as a product of and an agency in mainly its *own* national context. The connection with other literatures (in the discipline of comparative literature) is established mostly when there are some positive data to base it on, such as, say, influences of one work on another or shared poetics of a certain period or movement.

But one can also make numerous other connections among books coming from the various parts of the world—connections that take works away from the previously constructed contexts such as that of a work's national tradition or language or historical moment or genre—and read the work in the context created only in that particular idiosyncratic reading. After all, if we see reading as a much more active and free agency than merely discovering something that is already there, if reading is primarily a creation of something that is made through this activity, then connections made by the reader are plausible and make sense as long as they make sense in that particular reading. In other words, reading's creation of previously "nonexistent" connections entails the recognition of the free agency of not only writers and literature (Márquez learning from Kafka, Kundera admiring Rabelais and Rushdie, Kiš responding to Borges and Nabokov) but also reading and readers.

The last aspect of my book that I would like to address in this introduction is its use of the dialogue between literary works of different national origins. Making dialogues has to do with the possibility of reading to be creative, traveling freely across space and time, and making connections among literary works of various national origins, connections that do not have to have confirmation in "facts" outside of the particular act of reading. The three chapters of this book are organized in the form of dialogues between one Eastern European and one American or English literary work.

What is a dialogue? Two parties coming together, who through their conversation create something that neither of them knew before, something novel and unique. Without plunging into a discussion of the use of dialogue as a literary and philosophical mode par excellence, or into reflections on dialogue made by thinkers from Plato to Bakhtin, suffice it to say that, "educat[ing] each side about itself and about the other," a dialogue "not only discovers but activates potentials" of those who engage in it.[14] In other words, those involved in a dialogue do not only find out who their interlocutor is—and in relation to that who they themselves are—a dialogue helps both sides to move forward.

As I read certain Eastern European, English, and American books, I increasingly saw the existence of numerous dialogues and conversations—on many different subjects—which these books, coming from different places, held with each other.

I saw how Yugoslav writer Danilo Kiš's collection of stories *A Tomb for Boris Davidovich* engages in a dialogue on language with American John Cage's writings in *Silence;* I saw how Polish writer Tadeusz Borowski's stories in *This Way for the Gas, Ladies and Gentlemen* converse with British Kazuo Ishiguro's best-selling novel *The Remains of the Day* on the workings of power; and I saw Croatian Irena Vrkljan's autobiographical *Marina or About Biography* exploring issues of gender in a dialogue with American Susan Howe's *My Emily Dickinson.*

Let there be no mistake: these dialogues are not in the realm of the "factual." John Cage and Danilo Kiš, Tadeusz Borowski and Kazuo Ishiguro, and Irena Vrkljan and Susan Howe do not respond or refer to each other's work in any way, probably have not read each other's books and, to the best of my knowledge, have never said they knew of each other. Dialogues between their works are "ideal" ones, created by a reader who simultaneously reads these writers' books coming from different cultural contexts and who sees how these books are interconnected and implicated in each other, and how they—without knowing it—indeed talk to each other. These three imagined dialogues make up this book. Making imaginary dialogues lends more creative agency to reading itself, which does not only find and uncover connections that are presumably already there but rather makes those that do not exist unless made by the very act of reading.

Much English and American literature relates in diverse and unpredictable ways to the whole range of experiences, concerns, and themes present in Eastern Europe, and the reverse is also the case. The awareness of numerous potential dialogues among literary works coming from different places, as well as of relations and connections among these different places themselves, should enrich the sphere of knowledge and practice of each individual reader. Reading one literary work in dialogue with another from some other place shows how even seemingly unrelated things (books, places, people) are actually connected and implicated in each other—once a reader looks for and makes these connections.

Since being is being in the world with others, conversations—realized or potential—are always present. The relational reading of a literary work attempts to dissolve the solid borders between "us" and "them," borders defined nationally, linguistically, or culturally. That which is different from me, the foreign "other," is not an obstacle to my freedom but rather a potential extension and a missing part of me, which inspires me to move on, change, and explore novel ways of being that I could not find alone.

1

Literature against the Closures of Language: A Tomb for Boris Davidovich *by Danilo Kiš* and Silence *by John Cage*

> *No one can have an idea*
> 30″
> *once he starts really listening.*
> —John Cage, *Silence*

In this chapter, *A Tomb for Boris Davidovich* (*Grobnica za Borisa Davidoviča*, 1976), a collection of stories by Danilo Kiš on the revolutionaries and victims of Stalinist purges, converses with *Silence* (1961), an assortment of writings by American avant-garde artist, writer, and thinker John Cage. An Eastern European writer—a survivor of fascism, communism, and, in the last decades of his life, the "late capitalism" of 1980s France—engages in a dialogue on the closures and liberating potential of language with an American who defined the avant-garde art scene both in the United States and internationally and whom composer Arnold Schoenberg called "an inventor—of genius."

John Cage is a world-renowned artist who has decisively influenced the course not only of contemporary music, performance art, and avant-garde aesthetics but also of literature. In contrast, Danilo Kiš remains a somewhat unfamiliar name within the context of Eastern European literature that is known in the "West," since his "work has not brought him the sort of attention enjoyed in America by, say, Milan Kundera, Czeslaw Milosz, or Vaclav Havel. . . . Indeed, paradoxical confirmation of that fact was offered in 1990 when Kiš was posthumously awarded the Bruno Schulz Prize (given to a 'foreign writer underrecognized in the United States')."[1] Before proceeding with Kiš's dialogue with Cage, let me first say a few words about this "underrecognized" writer who still "lingers somewhere between repute and anonymity."[2]

Sketch of a Writer

Danilo Kiš was born in 1935 in the city of Subotica in Vojvodina, a province in northern Serbia, one of the republics of the former Yugoslavia. While central Serbia was occupied by the Ottoman Empire for centuries, Vojvodina was a part of Austria-Hungary. Thanks to its past, this area was characterized by a fabulous mixture of ethnicities, languages, and cultures inhabiting the former Hapsburg monarchy. Aside from the Hungarian, Serbian, Montenegrin, and Croatian populations (and many other smaller ethnic groups), Subotica at the time of Kiš's birth also had a sizable Jewish population, which was almost entirely liquidated during World War II, and a German population, which was largely expelled after the end of that war. In the intellectual and cultural history of the former Yugoslavia, Vojvodina is known, among other things, as the birthplace of Dositej Obradović, a major figure of the eighteenth-century Enlightenment. Obradović was a writer and a thinker, a teacher and traveler, whose cosmopolitan vision finds its late and strange echo in the writings of Danilo Kiš.

Kiš's father was a Hungarian Jew, his mother a Montenegrin. As a child, Kiš miraculously survived the massacre of Jews and Serbs carried out by Hungarian fascists in the city of Novi Sad in 1942. The family moved to Hungary; his father was taken to Auschwitz in 1944 and never returned. At the end of the war, Kiš and his mother returned to Yugoslavia, this time to the republic of Montenegro and the town of Cetinje, birthplace of his mother and the city of Petar Petrović Njegoš, a Montenegrin ruler and well-known nineteenth-century writer. When he arrived in Cetinje, Kiš "did not know many words of our [Serbo-Croatian] language. . . . This then unknown boy was called 'Madjar, Madjar' [Hungarian, Hungarian] and insulted."[3] Kiš quickly learned the language in which he was going to write all of his major works.

Kiš went on to study in Belgrade, where he was the first student to earn a degree from the newly created Department of Comparative Literature. He knew Hungarian, Russian, and French well and made translations from those languages. But following vituperative attacks by members of Yugoslavia's literary and political establishment in the 1970s, related to the publication of *A Tomb for Boris Davidovich*, Kiš permanently relocated to France.[4] He lived in Strasbourg, Bordeaux, Lille, and Paris and worked as a writer and a lecturer of the Serbo-Croatian language. He died of cancer in Paris in 1989 at the age of fifty-four.

Kiš's early works are usually referred to as a "family cycle." Poetic stories about a child growing up under the shadow of impending fascism comprise *Early*

Sorrows (*Rani jadi*, 1969). The novel *Garden, Ashes* (*Bašta, pepeo*, 1965), also taking Kiš's childhood as its theme, was characterized by the Russian poet and Nobel laureate Joseph Brodsky as "a veritable gem of lyrical prose, the best book produced on the Continent in the postwar period."[5] A dead father's newly discovered letter serves as the basis for *The Hourglass* (*Peščanik*, 1972). *Psalm 44* (*Psalam 44*, 1962) takes as its starting point a newspaper article reporting the postwar journey of a Jewish couple to the concentration camp where their child was born. The novel *Mansard* (*Mansarda*, 1962), a love story set in Belgrade, also belongs to this group of Kiš's early works.

How Can We Recognize a Metamorphosis of Evil?

In the early phase of his work, Kiš directly or indirectly dealt with past horrors— World War II, Auschwitz. However, he soon moved on. The question became: How can we recognize a metamorphosis of evil? In other words, past horrors like Auschwitz will not be repeated—not the same name, not the same people, not the same time. So paying homage to a fixed moment in history and saying that it shall not be repeated does not help much. That particular thing will certainly not be repeated—something else will happen that will take its place, somewhere else and at some other time, with different people and different ideologies, but with similar horrifying consequences.

Kiš characterized his sensing of "new evils" in physical terms: "One could say that I feel evil on my skin."[6] In pointing out the metamorphoses of horror, a fact that terror changes its appearance and name and thus cannot be recognized as a mere replica of something that has already happened, Kiš soon began to fight against "evil's" new embodiments, which, not recognized as such, had been gaining momentum. He fought on two fronts, within his two homelands—the former Yugoslavia and France.

In the context of the former Yugoslavia, Kiš opposed the rising nationalist discourse, which deemed that the mythologized past persecution of one nation justified an uncritical glorification of itself, as well as a dangerously paranoid view of other nations. Kiš sensed the "evil" in the transformation of nationalism from the means of preserving national identity in colonial times to an aggressive ideology. "Evil" nationalism takes the mythologized victimization of one's own nation in the past as a justification for that same nation's victimization of an alleged potential enemy in the future. Following the publication and success of *A Tomb for Boris Davidovich*, a smear campaign was launched against Kiš, accusing him of plagiarism but in effect "[aiming] to . . . dismiss him for his lack of national consciousness and insufficient affinity for the traditions of his milieu."[7] Subsequent to the ordeal of his battle against this campaign, Kiš made France his permanent place of residence.

In his aesthetics, Kiš also strongly opposed the notion of identity as built exclusively on one's national heritage, whereby the glorification of that heritage leads to a lack of understanding of and interest in other peoples and cultures. Opposing a national-based identity, Kiš promoted a cosmopolitan identity, one that is not "authentic but rather conjunctural," according to James Clifford, and that is based on multiple dialogues with others and on the notion that the identities of "others" and "ourselves" are not enclosed within such firm and well-defined boundaries as nationalists would have us think. These identities overlap or change each other by engaging in a dialogue, and we should thus think of their interaction not as external relation between closed firm bodies but rather as communication of multicentered spaces, whereby the centers of one space might also be the centers of another space. Kiš himself was described in anecdotal terms as "Belgradian by study and career, a Dubrovnik summer regular, French by literary education and exile, Russian when he recited poetry and told jokes."[8]

In his literary work, Kiš was influenced by writers from both the former Yugoslavia (Krleža, Crnjanski, Andrić) and abroad. In *A Tomb for Boris Davidovich*, one of Kiš's main literary interlocutors is Argentinean writer Jorge Luis Borges. Kiš used the Borgesian technique of "factual fiction," and he envisioned his book as a polemic with Borges's *Universal History of Infamy*. According to Kiš:

> [P]olemics is in the following: Borges names his most famous book *The Universal History of Infamy*; however, on a *thematic level*, this is not any universal history of infamy, but rather . . . stories for small children, socially entirely irrelevant, about New York gangsters, Chinese pirates, provincial criminals and so on. . . . And I claim that *the universal history of infamy* is the twentieth century with its camps, primarily Soviet ones. Because it is infamous when, in the name of an idea of a better world, for which generations of people gave their lives, when in the name of such a humanistic idea camps are created and their existence is hidden, and not only people but also their most human and intimate dreams about this better world are destroyed. The universal history of infamy can be reduced, therefore, to a destiny of all those unhappy idealists who went from Europe to the "Third Rome," to Moscow, and who were infamously and shamelessly drawn to a trap in which they would bleed and die like twice wounded animals.[9]

In his own country, Kiš opposed nationalism, xenophobia, political dogmatism, and aesthetic conservatism. In France, he opposed the 1970s leftist scene in what he saw as its inexcusably ignorant and apologetic view of Soviet communism and its crimes. Kiš wrote his *A Tomb for Boris Davidovich*, "seven chapters of the same history" of Stalinist purges, not only as a text that would participate in and shape the Yugoslav literary and political scene but also as a reaction to his stay in Bordeaux in the early 1970s.

> I lived in Bordeaux in the 1970s, at the time of the widespread "leftism" in France and in the West in general, when the fact of the Soviet camps was not yet accepted. One should not forget that Solzhenitsyn's book appears at approximately that time; however, in the first moment, the world refused to accept the terrible fact of the *Soviet* camps—whose existence is one of the crucial facts of this century—and thus leftist intellectuals did not even want to read this book, *The GULAG Archipelago,* considering it an act of ideological sabotage and rightist conspiracy. As one could not talk to these people on the level of general ideas, because they held aggressive opinions made a priori, I had to articulate my attitude in the form of anecdotes and stories. . . . These anecdotes remained a sole form of conversation which they could accept, in the sense of listening if not understanding. On the ideological, sociological or political level, these virtuous intellectuals did not bear any objection, because they were extremely intolerant and had grounded themselves in Manichaean concepts made a priori: East is Eden, West is Hell. . . . The existence of Soviet camps did not fit at all in their effortlessly made schemes. Therefore, they tried to close their eyes in front of the reality and not take this fact into consideration. . . . And those who had other references and nourished doubt, this Montaigne-like doubt and lucidity, like Aron in France, or Koestler and Poper in England, those were not only not listened to but were also rejected *en bloc* and a priori, as reactionaries, "bourgeois" thinkers, "fascists." . . . [T]hat was fanaticism, blindness and—arrogance.[10]

By turning his attention away from well-known crimes to ones that yet needed to be recognized as such, Kiš marks the main tenet of his poetic and ethic practice. One has to be able to recognize a "metamorphosis of evil" and to articulate this new evil with appropriately new literary means. In order to do so, one has to keep on changing one's preexistent ideas of good and evil and acknowledge that, for instance, "positive" nationalism helping people's survival in adversarial circumstances can turn into a murderous xenophobic ideology, just as a Communist ideology opposed to the inhumane world of capitalism can itself turn into the totalitarian nightmare of the Soviet camps.

Kiš's project of unceasing alertness to the changing forms of "evil," postulating critical elasticity of thinking and practice, can be understood as a struggle against epistemological and political "error [which is] a failure to adjust immediately from a preconception to an actuality," in the words of John Cage (*Silence,* 170). The French pro-Soviet left, unwilling to relinquish their idea of communism as a positive practice "by definition," regardless of its real embodiments, committed precisely this sort of error. As Kiš says, the existence of Soviet camps did not fit into their dogmas, so they tried to "close their eyes in front of reality and not take that fact [of the camps] into consideration." In short, they "failed to adjust." Certain concepts are appropriate in and for a certain context; when this particular context is changed, ideas need to be changed as well. Kiš's lifelong struggle consisted in the promotion of precisely such a flexibility and elasticity of thinking and practice.

Kiš and Cage: "A World without Art Would Not Be a Bad One"

In his lecture "Here Comes Everybody: Overpopulation and Art," John Cage talks about a "world without art," a world which would "not be bad."[11] In *Silence*, he writes:

what, precisely,   does this, this   beautiful profound object,   this masterpiece,
have to do   with Life?   It has this to do with Life   :   that it is
separate from it.   Now we see it   and now we don't.   When we see it
          we feel better, and when we are away from it, we don't feel so good
          . . . .
beautiful form suffices to brighten and throw light   upon mat-ters of lesser moment
          But important questions   cannot be decided
in this way   .   They require   greater earnestness

(130–31)

A world without art is a world in which there is no "beautiful form separated from life." It is a world in which art has been abolished. Or, art is art only in its abolishing, in existing as something which is not only a "beautiful form separated from life." The world in which art thus abolishes itself is "not a bad" one because art can abolish itself only by fully realizing itself in historical practice.

The works of Danilo Kiš and John Cage attempt to abolish themselves as "beautiful forms separated from life" and thus realize their "life" potential. The realization of these works is an ongoing possibility for every reader. "Useful" art, says Cage,

> should spill out of just being beautiful and move over to other aspects of life so that when we're not with the art it has nevertheless influenced our actions or our responses to the environment.[12]

The works of Kiš and Cage are very political in the sense of their potential to change the readers' intellectual landscape and thus inspire a different material practice. "[A]rt is a means of self-alteration, and what it alters is *mind*, and mind is in the world and is a social fact."[13] However, it is crucial to note that both Kiš and Cage resist programmatic political art. Cage says: "I have difficulty with it because it's so pushy. It has precisely in it what government has in it: the desire to control; and it leaves no freedom for me. It pushes me toward its conclusion. . . . The moment I hear that kind . . . I go in the opposite direction."[14]

Art with a "desire to control" and "leaving no freedom" cannot be liberating. Literature which represents and "pushes" any finite, fixed concept articulated outside of the literary work itself might propagate "the right ideas," but it does so in the wrong way, which makes genuine emancipation impossible. The point is not to control the reader's mind in order to change the "content" of it but rather to abet the self-liberation of this mind.

Kiš's and Cage's political art does not promote the notion of closures articulated outside of literature but rather makes us aware of other closures by reacting to them. Therefore, the reader cannot simply recognize familiar political notions and confirm or not confirm already existing beliefs. Instead, the reader can enable the art's "bringing into being" of different closures only by a "change of mind." "I think we are in a more urgent situation, where it is absolutely essential for us to change our minds fundamentally."[15]

Through the liberating reaction to the closures of language, the works of Kiš and Cage at the same time point at these closures and make us aware of them. A dialogue is here created in which *Silence* answers the question posed by *A Tomb for Boris Davidovich*, in which a question is a necessary part of the answer and vice versa, and in which both question and answer can be perceived as such only when juxtaposed one with the other.

A Tomb for Boris Davidovich

The Metaphor of the "Empty Tomb" and the Absence of History

History recorded him as Novsky, which is only a pseudonym (or, more precisely, one of his pseudonyms). But what immediately spawns doubt is the question: did history really *record* him? In the index of the *Granat Encyclopedia*, among the 246 authorized biographies and autobiographies of great men and participants in the Revolution, his name is missing. In his commentary on this encyclopedia, Haupt notes that all the important figures of the Revolution are represented, and laments only the "surprising and inexplicable absence of Podvoysky." Even he fails to make any allusion to Novsky, whose role in the Revolution was more significant than that of Podvoysky. So in a "surprising and inexplicable" way this man whose political principles gave validity to a rigorous ethic, this vehement internationalist, appears in the revolutionary chronicles as a character without a face or a voice.[16]

The loss or nonexistence of important texts is a recurrent theme in Kiš's writing. In the story "A Tomb for Boris Davidovich" quoted above, the entry for Boris Davidovich Novsky does not exist in Granat's *Encyclopedia of Revolutionaries*. In "Red Stamps with Lenin's Picture," a story in Kiš's *The Encyclopedia of the Dead* (1983), the letters of Jewish poet and revolutionary Mendel Osipovich are missing texts. Kiš's story "The Sow that Eats her Farrow" (*Tomb*, 17) is based on the absence of a text on Gould Verschoyle, an Irish volunteer fighting for the Republicans in the Spanish Civil War, who was briefly mentioned in one paragraph of Karlo Steiner's memoirs *Seven Thousand Days in Siberia*.[17]

Kiš's writing attempts to recover and reclaim lost texts. The famous line from Mikhail Bulgakov's *Master and Margarita* (1940), "manuscripts do not burn," could be one of the mottos of Kiš's opus. The frame of Kiš's writing is an assertion: there are texts that had once been actually or potentially written. These texts articulate points of collective history. They have been lost. I, a writer, am finding and presenting them, thus making these lost texts communal again.[18]

For Danilo Kiš, the writer's vocation is to understand what texts are lost (that is, what texts are missing and why), and then to "rewrite" them. The title story from Kiš's *The Encyclopedia of the Dead*, for example, presents itself as only a "retelling" of one entry from the "just found" *Encyclopedia of the Dead*.[19] Kiš's project of "finding and rewriting" lost texts that were never written can be described by the following reflection from Christa Wolf's *The Quest for Christa T.*: "one cannot . . . cling to the facts. . . . *one has to invent, for the truth's sake*."[20]

After noting the absence of Boris Davidovich Novsky from Granat's *Encyclopedia of Revolution*, Kiš's story "A Tomb for Boris Davidovich" proceeds:

> The ancient Greeks had an admirable custom: for anyone who perished by fire, was swallowed by a volcano, buried by lava, torn to pieces by beasts, devoured by sharks, or whose corpse was scattered by vultures in the desert, they built so-called cenotaphs, or empty tombs, in their homelands; for the body is only fire, water, or earth, whereas the soul is the Alpha and the Omega, to which a shrine should be erected. (*Tomb*, 74)

The body of a unique reality—or a very particular human body—is gone, disappearing into nothingness and leaving no trace behind it. The empty tomb made of stones is built as a sign, a mark of that vanished past. A writer living in the present cannot re-create past realities. However, s/he can now create the empty tombs of these realities, cenotaphs that had not been built in the past. The writer re-creates the lost history, as well as points out the fact that it had been lost, by reclaiming that history's texts/signs, that is, by making now empty tombs for the lost past.

The creation of community is aided by an understanding of collective history. Kiš wants to reclaim some aspects of this history by "bringing into being" the missing tombs/texts. In order to make these newly created texts relevant, Kiš has to oppose the ironic dismissal of the possibility of these texts. I shall later write at length about this irony as a cultural feature that has characterized the Eastern European public landscape. Suffice it to say now that Kiš articulates irony as a cultural "closure" through reacting to it. This reaction lies in Kiš's reclaiming of the anti-ironic referentiality, which allows his texts to truly "speak" the presently missing but once existing history.

Reclaiming Language Referentiality

Biblical Creation of the World

My mother read the novels until she was twenty, when she discovered, not without sadness, that novels were only fiction, and she rejected them altogether. Her aversion to "pure invention" had a latent birth in me.[21]

The wedding ceremony was performed on December 27, 1919, on the torpedo boat Spartacus, which was anchored in Kronstadt harbor. . . . The boat was quickly decorated with signal flags and lit up with red, green, and blue bulbs. Simultaneously celebrating the wedding and their victory over death, the crew appeared on deck freshly shaved and pink cheeked, fully armed, as if for an inspection. But the cables informing the general staff about the course of operation and the lucky rescue had drawn the attention of the officers of the Red fleet, who now arrived in blue military overcoats over their white summer uniforms. The torpedo boat greeted them with whistles and the cheers of the crew. The breathless radioman brought to the commander's bridge, where the young married couple had taken shelter, uncoded cables with congratulations from all the Soviet ports from Astrakhan to Enzeli: "Long live the newlyweds!" "Long live the Red fleet!" "Hurrah for the brave crew of the Spartacus!" The Revolutionary Council of Kronstadt sent armored cars with nine cases of French champagne seized from the anarchists the day before. Kronstadt's brass band climbed up the gangplank and onto the deck playing marches. Because of the temperature, 22° below zero (Fahrenheit), the instruments had a strange, cracked sound, as if made of ice. (*Tomb*, 86–87)

The above paragraph (on the marriage ceremony between the revolutionaries Boris Davidovich Novsky and Zinaida Mihailovna Maysner) displays an accumulation of precise details and the rhythm of sentence and narration which re-creates a rhythm of the described event.[22] These features characterize Kiš's intense and "accurate" imagining—and narrating—of another, distant time and place.[23] His imaginative power and the skill with which he uses his "poetics of detail" help his stories literally "set up a world" of the revolutionaries in the 1930s.[24] In order for the lost world and missing history to be re-created through language, Kiš needs to achieve a referential (rather than self- or nonreferential) language. Kiš attains this referential language by reenacting the ways in which the Bible's language creates the world. In *Garden, Ashes*, Kiš writes:

> The book of my life, the book that had such a profound and far-reaching effect on me, the book from which my nightmares and fantasies were recruited . . . was the *Small School Bible* . . . the divine conciseness of the anecdote, this essence of essences stripped of eloquence, these events bared to the bone, this story line brought to the white heat. . . .
>
> I suffered in my childhood the destinies of all the Old Testament personages, the sins of the sinners and the righteousness of the righteous, I was by turns Cain and Abel, I was idling on Noah's ark and drowning in the sea with the sinful. *People had become more and more numerous and were full of iniquities. God then said to Noah: Build yourself an ark, for I am going to flood the entire earth.* . . .
>
> I experienced this Biblical drama of the flood as my own personal drama. . . . Once the water recedes and the ark has touched the earth . . . I mix my shouting with the shouting of those getting off the ark, I gaze upon the triumphal flight of the birds streaking out of their cages, I listen to their singing, I listen to the roaring of the lions who are leaving claw marks in the still moist, cracked earth, I listen to the deafening thud of the hoofed creatures that are trampling soil sprouting freshly with grasses and flowers, new onions and sorrel, while the figs and oranges just brought onto land are bursting like berries, swollen with the weight of their juices and their role in life.[25]

The Bible's language creates the world: a reader gazes at the birds' triumphal flight, sees the claw marks which the lions leave in the still moist earth, listens to the beasts roar and birds sing. The ability of biblical language to create the world, this linguistic referentiality articulated as the most substantial language characteristic in Kiš's *Garden, Ashes*, is reenacted in *A Tomb for Boris Davidovich*. Moments from the past world (such as the one of Novsky's marriage cited above) are created in front of the reader's eyes by the absolute imagination, which speaks with the language of prophets. As Karl-Markus Gauss writes: "Kiš attempts to make a destroyed world so fully present in language that this world not only gets restored; it is created again. The literary archaeologist Kiš here becomes the creator of the world."[26]

Documentary Techniques

The Bible's language, speaking of the creation of the world and history, is highly referential. By his own rendition of this quality of the Bible's language, Kiš himself attains a referentiality which re-creates missing history. However, this referentiality of Kiš's stories and the "truthful" character of his biographies of revolutionaries is also achieved by another literary device: by Kiš's writing a "'documentary' fiction or faction."[27] As Branko Gorjup points out, "Kiš's fiction makes use of documentary material in two distinct ways. First, most of the plots in the work are derived or borrowed from already existing sources of varied literary significance, some easily recognizable—for example, those extracted from Roy Medvedev and Karl Steiner—while others are more obscure. Second, Kiš employs the technique of textual transposition, whereby entire sections or series of fragments, often in their unaltered state, are taken from other texts and freely integrated into the fabric of his work."[28]

Kiš's stories cite numerous primary and secondary sources of information—both authentic and false—on particular revolutionaries. These citations are often placed in footnotes together with the author's comments. Throughout his writing, the author reflects abundantly on the use of these sources in his attempts to reconstruct the imperfect but best possible chronology of the events. Consider, for example, the passage "Faded Photographs" from the story "The Sow That Eats Her Farrow." This story is a biography of Gould Verschoyle, an Irish volunteer in the Spanish Republican Army, who was kidnapped and prosecuted by the Soviets.

Here the reliability of the documents, resembling, as they do, palimpsests, is suspended for a moment. The life of Gould Verschoyle blends and merges with the life and death of the young Spanish Republic. We have only two snapshots. One, with an unknown soldier next to the ruins of a shrine. On the back, in Verschoyle's handwriting: "Alcázar. Viva la República." His high forehead is half covered by a Basque beret, a smile hovers around his lips, on which one can read (from today's perspective) the triumph of the victor and the bitterness of the defeated: the paradoxical reflections that, like a line on the forehead, foreshadow inevitable death. Also, a group snapshot with the date November 5, 1936. The picture is blurred. Verschoyle is in the second row, still with a Basque beret pulled over his forehead. In front of the lined-up group a landscape stretches out, and it would not be hard to believe that we are in a cemetery. Is this the Honor Guard that fired salvos in

the sky or into living flesh? The face of Gould Verschoyle jealously guards
this secret. Over the rows of soldiers' heads, in the distant blue an airplane
hovers like a crucifix. (*Tomb*, 20)

In his polemical *The Anatomy Lesson*, Kiš writes: "This persistent, I could even
say maniacal insisting on document, witnessing, fact, citation . . . could by itself
be a sufficient indication that a writer obviously wants to emphasize the meaning
of his/her literary device, whose ultimate goal is to convince the reader of the
truthfulness of these stories, truthfulness of described events."[29] "In the book *A
Tomb for Boris Davidovich* many sources are cited, authentic and false . . . and names,
authentic and false . . . in this world of fiction where the truthful and false mix,
in this world of literary mystification—whose ultimate goal, paradoxically, is the
attainment of some objective, *historical truth.*"[30]

Both Kiš's "biblical" language re-creating the world of revolutionaries, on
one hand, and his "maniacal insisting on document," on the other hand, aim to
attain "some objective, *historical truth.*" Kiš's stories presuppose and are based on the
possibility of their own "truth value" or referentiality, the ability of stories to be
not "only" fiction but also to articulate or refer to something "outside" of them, the
past material reality that indeed took place. As such, Kiš's stories are "invention for
the truth's sake." "(O)ne cannot . . . cling to the facts. . . . one has to invent, for
the truth's sake."[31] Or as the beginning of *A Tomb for Boris Davidovich* puts it:

The story I am about to tell, a story born in doubt and perplexity, has only
the misfortune (some call it fortune) of being true. (3)

As mentioned earlier, the referentiality of Kiš's stories is literature's reaction
to a specific cultural "closure" which is itself articulated, or "brought into being,"
precisely by literature's reaction to it. This cultural closure lies in the dismissal of
the possibility of the referentiality of texts dealing with topics such as revolution.
This closure, in short, is one of absolute irony. In order to successfully re-create the
missing "empty tombs" (texts) and the lost collective history, Kiš's referentiality
has to encounter and oppose the absolute ironic dismissal of the possibility of such
texts.

Living in Lie and the "Bad Infinity" of Endless Irony

Irony that dismisses the possibility of relevant, "truthful" texts on topics such as,
for example, "revolution" or "socialism" was a direct public reaction to Eastern
European Communist societies' "living in lie." In Václav Havel's essay "Power of
the Powerless or Living in Truth," the word "lie" refers to the utmost discrepancy

between the official "public" language and reality. This discrepancy creates "a formalized language deprived of semantic contact with reality and transformed into a system of ritual signs that replace reality with pseudo-reality."[32] Every instance of official text is marked by this "lack of semantic contact" with reality. Words, phrases, and whole texts signify different or even exactly opposite meanings to their directly referential ones. Thus, "honest" means corrupted, "revolutionary" means co-opted and opportunistic, and an "enemy" is someone who is trying to improve things, and so on.

Much Eastern European literature takes as its theme this discrepancy between words and reality in "living in lie." In Czech writer Zdena Salivarová's novel *Summer in Prague* (1971), for instance, the narrator and main character of the novel, the young and independently minded singer Jana Honzlová discovers by chance the official dossier on herself and her family. This document describes Jana's parents in the following way:

> Honzlová's father is a former capitalist exploiter of the working classes. Her mother is a former "lady of leisure" who used to kick her maids in the old days. Nowadays she walks around Karlin publicly abusing our socialist democratic system.[33]

After displaying this official text, Jana proceeds with a description of her family's real social circumstances, thus creating a comic discrepancy between the reality and the above official naming of it:

> I must admit that my mother did criticize the National Fruit and Vegetable Enterprise store fairly often and quite indiscriminately for being out of onions, but I'm certain she never went so far as to express herself in public about our socialist democratic system. Comments of that nature she saved for home. She had learned from past experience. And as for Father, during the time of the Republic he made a living selling soaps, contraceptives, laundry and cleaning supplies in his neighborhood drug store, in today's view wrongfully growing rich by oppressing the poor workers. He didn't work. He only sold. Mother cleaned the shop.
> But once when she had a big belly yet again, so huge she couldn't manage to put on her shoes, Father hired a maid. But she ran away from us the very next day because the bedbugs that crawl to our house from the Manases' nearly ate her alive the first night. Mother didn't have to kick her. The maid ran off on her own steam straight to the doctor's with her bites, and Mr. Druggist had to pay her hush money as well as give her an ointment for the bite, to keep her from yelling about it all over the neighborhood and

chasing away customers. She yelled nevertheless, so that even his business suffered as a result of his bourgeois extravagances.[34]

Jana Honzlová's brother Hugo is injured in the collapse of the balcony of the family's apartment. The official text on the accident, appearing in the daily paper, reads as follows:

Tragic Consequences of Negligence

Yesterday two old balconies at 26 Zizkov Street in Karlin collapsed and fell, seriously injuring ten-year-old H.H. and fifty-year-old J.T. The tenants of the building neglected to inform the District Housing Bureau in time of the critical condition of the balconies. As a result of her fellow tenants' negligence, J.T. has paid with her life. Critically injured H.H. continues to fight for his life.[35]

Jana counterposes the factual account of "family negligence" to the above report, again marking a discrepancy between the true situation and its official text:

"Mother reported it to the District Housing Bureau I don't know how many times, many, many times. The latest time was last Friday. But they almost kicked her out, telling her we should prop it up ourselves."[36]

Writing about rituals of public speech in Communist Eastern Europe, Václav Havel asserts that their main characteristic was a reproduction of the same well-known lies. Public life became a travesty, a theater of simulation. Havel designates "living in truth," that is, any instance of truthfulness (be it a good poem or well-done work), as a main locus of oppositional activity.[37]

In the Eastern European Communist "world of lie," words like "socialism," "capitalism," "bourgeoisie," "history," "revolution," and so on, stood as labels of a state-approved or nonapproved position. In *Summer in Prague*, we read: "If they [the rulers] don't like a person then he's bourgeois [i.e., the wealthy capitalist exploiter and "enemy of the people"], even if he grew up eating stone soup."[38] Words such as "bourgeoisie" (or "revolution," "justice," "truth," and many others) are stripped of their previous more "immanent" meanings. Talking about the ruining of "once beautiful" words, Jana Honzlová says:

If I were a poet I'd make up beautiful words having no sense other than being melodious and sounding like newly discovered chords; yldam, Helimadoe, Aminadab, I'd make a sort of dictionary of beautiful words, a precious, secret gift for my friends, so that people like Farajzl, say, couldn't get those beautiful words in their mouths to ruin them, a fate that has befallen so many other once-beautiful words.[39]

Having been used for the creation of the official power discourse that produces "living in lie," the "once-beautiful words" got "ruined." These words have lost their referents and are now used only for the formulaic realization of the rules of a specific official genre, such as political speech, newspaper article, production report, or biography of a revolutionary.

The political system's "ruin" or travesty of "once-beautiful words" causes an ironic and skeptical public reception of them.[40] The public's irony is a reaction to the loss of referentiality—irony functions as a stance of acknowledgment that words do not mean what they are supposed to. This irony now sees the words and their texts only as overused, wasted phrases that do not refer to anything any more. Words like "history" or "revolution" are so overused (and "abused") within a power discourse that they become—in the ironic public eye—simulacra, words emptied of their referents. Kiš thus writes his biographies of revolutionaries in a cultural context in which many official biographies of acknowledged revolutionaries are met—and instantly dismissed—with great irony.

The ironic public reception "knows" that these words are not what they are supposed to be. But this irony also loses the notion of what these words, names, or concepts should or could be about. "Revolution," having become a sheer label for the police state, has lost any other past or potential meaning. This word, along with many other words and texts, has lost its other referents due to the related forces of power discourse, on one hand, and the recipient's irony, on the other. Irony toward a power discourse empties the words and texts of their intended ideological meanings but does not give other meanings or referents instead. Rather, it simply puts away those words and texts.

Writing about the ironic "space between the lines" in Eastern European "oppositional" literature of the Communist period, Hungarian dissident Miklós Haraszti claims: "So even when we are critical between the lines, we never try to hide there anything we would express had it been allowed. Actually, we have no idea what our message would be if it could be freely articulated."[41] Irony functions as a constantly critical, negative force, displacing all the intended connections between signs and their signifieds. It is a resistance in its negativity of always postulating that something is not as it is said to be. Absolute irony, however, endlessly displaces any possibility of "positive" knowledge and related referential language: "we have no idea what our message would be if it could be freely articulated."

Irony can be seen as a "Hegelian 'bad' infinity."[42] It is a "reflectiveness [that] negates immediacy, but thereby shatters it to an infinite indeterminacy . . . irony raises the subject out of its mindless communion with the world, critically un-hinging it from the real; but . . . it yields no positive alternative truth."[43] This "positive alternative truth" does not have to be a dogma devoid of its own self-alteration. The main point in regard to irony's "infinite indeterminacy," however, is that the "truth is [not] 'indeterminate'; it is quite determinate enough. . . . As such, it can [not] be encompassed. . . . by the dogmatism of an endless deconstructive irony."[44]

The Closure of Absolute Irony

But, on the other hand, let us not forget that in the specific example of the stories from A Tomb for Boris Davidovich we talk about the "historical novel," historical material, stories in whose truthfulness a writer wants to convince the reader.[45]

In A Tomb for Boris Davidovich, Danilo Kiš wants to reclaim missing history, that is, the missing "empty tombs," texts that thematize certain topics crucial for the understanding of history, topics such as "revolution," "revolutionary," and so on. But the endless deconstructive irony present in public reception dismisses the possibility of any relevant speech on these topics. Thus, in order to create his cenotaph for revolutionary Boris Davidovich, Kiš has to dismantle this prevailing public irony itself. Kiš's language practice that opposes (and through that also "fleshes out") the closure of irony, is the practice of language referentiality.

The "empty tomb" is the text that circumscribes a material reality now missing but present at some point in the past. Absolute irony, on the contrary, would see "empty tomb" as Baudrillard's simulacra, a text (thematizing, in this case, a topic of a "revolutionary") that is entirely "empty" and nonreferential, rather than a text which points out that the lost material referent did indeed exist in the past.[46] Kiš's collection of short stories articulates and goes against the closure of absolute irony as the closure of this frozen belief in "simulacra."

A Tomb for Boris Davidovich engages this ironic distance from the referential use of language, this "disbelief in language." The book attempts to reverse the process by which material reality becomes only an overused textuality. Kiš tries to go against the process in which certain words and topics got so travestied within a power discourse that they became simulacra, images without referents. A Tomb for Boris Davidovich tries to find a way for language to again be able to "bring reality into being," as Heidegger would put it, and alert and wake readers up from the linguistic and cognitive apathy and cynicism they found themselves in because of what was happening to language in Eastern European Communist systems.

Kiš wants to bring back non-self-de(con)structive, nonironic language. He wants to narrate things such as revolution, socialism, and revolutionary biographies, which have been completely contaminated by their overusage in the power discourse. Kiš sees these things as having been taken away from readers because they are always present in their petrified transformation in the symbols of power, so ubiquitous that one ceases to even see them, let alone wonder about them.

In other words, the reclaimed referentiality of *A Tomb for Boris Davidovich* is an aspect of a construction, as opposed to a deconstruction, of a language and its referent, which is in this case a collective history. This "constructive" language of referentiality reacts to the closure of a deconstructed ironic (negative) language, brought about by "living in lie." However, Kiš's stories cannot reclaim any plausible referentiality by fully excluding the ironic moment of language. Rather, these stories negate irony by preserving it as a "mastered" moment of a referentiality itself, or as a self-transcended "committed irony."

"Committed" Irony and the Myth of Revolution

Ironic Referentiality

Opposing absolute irony in his attempted creation of the referentiality of his stories, Kiš, at the same time, retains the ironic stance toward narration itself.[47] Kiš admired Vladimir Nabokov, Boris Pilynak, Bruno Schulz, and Jorge Luis Borges, as well as theorists such as Shklovskii, Barthes, and Foucault. He also lived in the context of absolute irony. He knew that he could not attain the referentiality of his stories by erasing their "constructedness," the fact that they are made in specific ways by a specific author rather than "transmitted" from the sphere of absolute knowledge by an omniscient narrator. The referentiality of Kiš's time thus has to include the ironic "baring of devices" of literary construction, the admittance rather than the erasure of this "artificiality" of literary texts. Therefore, Kiš's stories display a marked presence of the narrator and a high consciousness of the constructedness of the text. Consider, for example, the following passage from the story "The Mechanical Lions":

> So I will tell the story of that encounter of long ago between Chelyustnikov and Herriot as well as I can, freeing myself for a moment of that awful burden of documents in which the story is buried, while referring the skeptical and curious reader to the appended bibliography, where he will find the necessary proof. (Perhaps it would have been wiser if I had chosen some other form of expression—an essay or a monograph—where I could use all these documents in the usual way. Two things, however, prevent me: the inappropriateness of citing actual oral testimony of reliable people as documentation; and my inability to forgo the pleasure of narration, which allows the author the deceptive idea that he is creating the world and thereby, as they say, changing it.) (*Tomb*, 31)

The ironic rhetoric of Kiš's stories lies in their "baring of (literary) devices" and in the stance of the narrator who "admits" that he does not create or simply "show" the world like an omniscient narrator of realism. Rather, this narrator retells the already written body of insufficient, imperfect, and often contradictory texts on the subject.[48] The ironic narrator of Kiš's biographies is an outsider who constructs the flawed chronology of events on the basis of evidence that is also present or referred to in the text. The stories fashion themselves as collages made out of concise summaries of or direct citations from previously existing texts taken as pieces of evidence. These stories are self-reflective attempts to construct chronologies of events. Thus, biographies of revolutionaries do not appear as finished constructions with absent traces of the ways in which they were made, but rather as necessarily imperfect attempts to construct. The referentiality itself of these stories is thus also imperfect—and is only possible as imperfect—but not nonexistent.

> The crew was strewn all over the deck as if dead, lying on heaps of broken glass, empty bottles, confetti, and small frozen puddles of French champagne rosy as blood. (The reader recognizes, surely, the awkward lyricism of Leo Mikulin, a student of the Imagists.)
>   . . . . . . but one reporter observed the absence of zeal, and the dull gaze . . .
>   . . . On the basis of very recent information, given by A. L. Rubina, Novsky's sister, this is what happened later. (87–89)

Chronicle Rather Than History

Opposing absolute irony, Kiš creates his referentiality by retaining some irony in the form of his postmodern ironic consciousness of literary construction. Necessary for the creation of plausible referentiality, this preserved and "transcended" irony is also present in Kiš's articulation of one of the most important elements of the revolutionaries' biographies. This crucial element is the moment in which men and women became revolutionaries in the first place. Irony in Kiš's articulation of one's becoming a revolutionary lies in the construction of this biographical turning point according to the principles of chronicle rather than history.

Hayden White asserts that the main difference between a chronicle and a history lies in the absence (chronicle) or presence (history) of the explicated causality of events. Something happens because of a certain cause or "overall scheme of things" in a history. A chronicle's irony toward this or that causality or "overall scheme of things" creates the situation in which something "simply happens." In opposition to history proper, ironic chronicles do not construct "any necessary connection between one event and another."[49] These events "are apparently as incomprehensible as natural events. . . . They seem merely to have occurred."[50] The mode of a chronicle is one of parataxis, as Erich Auerbach would put it, or the mode of additive time of "and then, and then, and then . . . ," and not the mode of causality or "hypotaxis."

The mode of Kiš's articulation of one's becoming a revolutionary is that of a chronicle, a narrative "parataxis" ("what happened next") that does not display any apparent causality. Kiš's "chronicle" technique thus retains an ironic stance toward any transparent causality of events. The narrator does not write about, for example, the "psychological motivations" of observed revolutionaries and does not present any text in which the revolutionaries themselves talk about or explain their path to becoming revolutionaries. Reading about the lives of Boris Davidovich Novsky or Karl Taube, one finds a lot about the period prior to their revolutionary activity. But then, "due to the absence of reliable documents," there is no text that directly or indirectly thematizes exactly why these two decided to choose the path of revolution, why they became—of all the things one supposes they could have become—revolutionaries.

In a letter to his fiancée, Zinaida Mihailovna Maysner, Boris Davidovich Novsky writes: "My only passion was this arduous, rapturous, and mysterious profession of revolutionary" (*Tomb*, 85–86). But nowhere in this letter or anywhere else does Novsky thematize the reasons or origins of becoming a revolutionary. Kiš's chronicles describe to a certain extent places and backgrounds from which revolutionaries had come. But these backgrounds, diverse as they are (the well-to-do pharmacist's son, Karl Taube, from "The Magic Card Dealing" versus, for example, poor Miksha from "The Knife with the Rosewood Handle") do not provide a sufficiently homogeneous "social" or any other cause for becoming revolutionaries, and not something else, in the first place.

"Pictures from the Album," a part of the story "The Magic Card Dealing," ends with young Karl Taube departing by train from Budapest to Vienna, waving goodbye to his father. The next part of the story (titled "Credo") begins with the sentence: "Two important factors prevent a better understanding of this tumultuous period in the life of Karl Taube: his illegal activities and the numerous aliases he used" (57). There is no explanation of the missing link—of the reasons or even specific ways in which Taube became the perpetrator of these "illegal activities" in the first place. The chapter then proceeds to describe Taube's revolutionary activity.

In a similar way, the title story "A Tomb for Boris Davidovich" renders Novsky's transformation from a worker to a revolutionary with a single sentence: "In February 1913 we find him in Baku as a fireman's helper on a steam engine; in September of the same year, among the leaders of a strike in a wallpaper factory in Ivanovo-Voznesenk; in October, among the organizers of the street demonstrations in St. Petersburg" (77). Again, no explanation is given as to why this change happened.

Myth of Revolution

In his *The Theory of the Novel*, Georg Lukács writes how the medieval chivalrous novel needed the unquestioned presence of a transcendental god for its very existence. This transcendence provided a guarantor of the narrative. In the medieval novel, things happen the way they do because there is this transcendental level (a God) which makes these narratives not only possible but also inevitable. Thus, a knight in these novels will always end up winning despite "realistic" odds to the contrary, and his story could not be an unbelievable fiction because it is written and read against the background of the presence of God in the world. Since it is inevitable, the knight's narrative is also always the same.

The biographies of Boris Davidovich Novsky or doctor Karl Taube, a Hungarian revolutionary from "The Magic Card Dealing," create the effect of a similar transcendental presence which is never directly written about but which functions as the basic condition of the narrative. These biographies are based on the presence of a mythical underlying structure which makes one's becoming a revolutionary not only possible but inevitable. There is no explanation as to exactly why the characters become revolutionaries because the stories attempt to re-create a world in which there is no sufficient "reason" or cause for this to happen. Becoming a revolutionary is as inevitable as the knight's victory in chivalrous novels, because this becoming takes place in a world captured by myth—the myth of revolution.

The revolutionaries in Kiš's stories are constituted on the background of this myth, which functions as an unavoidable presence that inevitably enacts itself in each individual narrative. In becoming revolutionaries, Kiš's characters are manifestations of a material force of this powerful myth. The subjects of revolution and of Kiš's stories thus lose individuality to an extent because the presence of the same mythic base that forms the particular biographies makes all the biographies of revolutionaries inevitable and equivalent.

In mythic homogenization, any place is any other place and anyone is any other one: the Russian Boris Davidovich Novsky is thus equated with the Hungarian Karl Taube or the Pole Hanna Krzyzewska. The myth of revolution functions as a whirlpool, drawing into its vortex countless individuals from various spheres of life and different geographical regions. The myth of revolution thus accounts for the inevitability of the revolutionaries' becoming revolutionaries in the first place. Regardless of whether one is, for example, a well-off Hungarian, a poor Romanian, or "bourgeois" Pole, one ends up in the same way. The unspoken mythical background of Kiš's stories characterizes the historical moment in which "becoming a revolutionary" was for many not so much a choice but a fate.

The myth of revolution as a basis for Kiš's stories can be seen as a compound of the myths of rational history (provenance of Hegel) and the approaching revolution (provenance of Marx). In Marx's words, "Philosophy becomes a material force when it grasps the masses." Hegel's and Marx's philosophies become material force through their transformation into the myth of history and revolution. In Kiš's stories, this myth is articulated through a cumulation of biographies whose subjects, despite individual differences, all enact the unspoken transcendental mythic presence which makes becoming a revolutionary a fate.[51]

The most "distinguished" and also most individual revolutionaries, such as Karl Taube and Boris Davidovich Novsky, start resisting the myth of revolution at some point in their biographies. After coming to Moscow in 1935, Taube acknowledges the falseness of the Soviet revolution, while Novsky asserts his truth against the myth of never failing revolutionary justice during his interrogation. However, even in the case of these two revolutionaries' biographies, the power of the myth of revolution is present (solely but decisively) in the inevitability and fate of their becoming revolutionaries in the first instance.

Pictures from the Album

Karl Georgievich Taube was born in 1899 in Esztergom, Hungary. Despite the meager data covering his earliest years, the provincial bleakness of the Middle European towns at the turn of the century emerges clearly from the depths of time: the gray, one-story houses with black yards that the sun in its slow journey divides with a clear line of demarcation into quarters of murderous light and damp, moldy shade resembling darkness; the rows of black locust trees, which at the beginning of spring exude, like thick cough syrups and cough drops, the musky smell of childhood diseases; the cold, baroque gleam of the pharmacy where the Gothic of the white porcelain vessels glitters; the gloomy high school with the paved yard (green, peeling benches, broken swings resembling gallows, and whitewashed wooden out-houses); the municipal building painted Maria-Theresa yellow, the color of the dead leaves and autumn roses from ballads played at dusk by the gypsy band in the open-air restaurant of the Grand Hotel.

Like so many provincial children, the pharmacist's son, Karl Taube, dreamed about that happy day when, through the thick lenses of his glasses, he would see his town from the bird's-eye view of departure and for the last time, as one looks through a magnifying glass at dried-out and absurd yellow butterflies from one's school collection: with sadness and disgust.

In the autumn of 1920, at Budapest's Eastern Station he boarded the first-class car of the Budapest-Vienna Express. The moment the train pulled out, the young Karl Taube waved once more to his father (who was disappearing like a dark blot in the distance, waving his silk handkerchief), then quickly carried his leather suitcase into the third-class car and sat down among the workers. (*Tomb*, 56)

The world of Taube's birthplace is one of dried-out yellow butterflies, alive and meaningful in some unknown past, and now dead and absurd for a long time.[52] The tone of "Pictures from the Album" makes it clear that a young man like Karl Taube, well-read ("glasses"), middle-class (a "pharmacist's son," "silk handkerchief," "leather bag"), and dreaming about "departure," has to turn his back to this dead world. The unspoken presence of the myth of revolution enfolds Taube's biography. In the 1920s, the "way out" for many appears to be only on the express train (revolution), from the Eastern Station (Russia), and with the presumed carriers of the revolution, workers (third-class passengers), who, "by abolishing themselves, [will] abolish the whole class society" (Marx).

The Myth of the Fully Known World and of the Achieved Knowledge of How to Act

Opposing the cultural closure of absolute irony, which dismisses any meaningful speech on revolution, Kiš's *A Tomb for Boris Davidovich* creates the anti-ironic referentiality of words such as "revolution" and "revolutionary." This referentiality, however, includes in itself what I call here a "committed irony," the text's awareness of its own constructedness. This paradoxical "ironic referentiality" is also characterized by the narration of revolutionaries' biographies according to the rules of chronicle rather than history. Events are narrated chronologically, without attempts to find and spell their mutual causality. The chronicle mode allows the articulation of a situation in which there is no particular individual cause or reason for becoming a revolutionary. The absence of a specific individual causality shows that becoming a revolutionary was a given, common biographical turn in certain times. This commonality transpires the presence of the powerful myth of revolution, which explains why people become revolutionaries. In a world captured by this myth, becoming a revolutionary is an inevitable fate.

Opposing the closure of absolute irony, Kiš encounters and articulates another closure, that of myth. In the title story, "A Tomb for Boris Davidovich," Kiš reacts to the closure of myth by microscopically enlarging it and showing precisely how it worked. The struggle of Boris Davidovich Novsky to shape the text of his own confession is the struggle for liberating knowledge, crucial for the future of Kiš's time and beyond, against the closure of mythic thinking and practice. Given that the myth involving the world of *A Tomb for Boris Davidovich* is that of revolution, one could think that Kiš's opposition to this would be completely irrelevant for the contemporary post-Communist world. However, Kiš's narrative "analysis" of this myth shows that its mechanism contains elements that are more than present—and more than dangerous and destructive—in current times as well.

Hegelian Triad

1. Texts That Interpret the World: The Thesis

The chronology of Boris Davidovich Novsky's life spells out three distinct ways of "being in the world." The first is being through words and language, through those texts that Boris Davidovich read, heard, or produced himself. After the paragraph about Boris Davidovich's probable birth dates, the first part of the story directly concerned with his life begins with the sentence: "At the age of four he was already able to read and write" (76). This significant beginning of life, this reading and writing and the presence of diverse literature that Davidovich absorbed or made himself, decisively mark the first modus of his relating to the world.

> [A]t nine his father took him along to the Saratov Tavern. . . . The place was frequented by retired soldiers . . . as well as by converted Jewish merchants. . . . Since he was already more literate than his father, little Boris Davidovich recorded their complaints. In the evening, they say, his mother read the Psalms to him, chanting them. When he was ten, an old estate overseer told him about the peasant uprisings of 1846: a harsh tale in which the knout, saber and gallows dealt out both justice and injustice. (76)

The texts of Boris Davidovich's childhood—complaints of soldiers and merchants, Psalms, stories about the people's bloody uprisings, the texts of social injustice and human suffering—are followed by other carefully recorded readings: "[A]t seventeen, as a dock worker in Riga, [Boris Davidovich is] reading Leonid Andreyev and Scheller-Mihaylov while out on strike" (77). Later on in his life, having been "again sentenced" because of the organization of a "secret terrorist group among the prisoners," Boris Davidovich reads "Antonio Labriola's texts on historical materialism" (78). In his confinement, "in the shadow of the gallows," he "listened to the screams and last words of those being led to their death" (78). Still later, free and in Paris, "we find him in the Russian Library on the Avenue des Gobelins and in the Musée Guimet, where he studied the philosophy of history and religion" (82).

Novsky is not only a passionate reader and listener of texts and words, he is himself a prolific writer and speaker, a conversationalist and an agitator. He edits *Eastern Dawn,* "printed on cigarette paper in a secret printing shop" (80), collaborates in Berlin "on the Social Democratic *Neue Zeitung* and *Leipziger Volkzeitung,*" and writes "among other things . . . a famous review of Max Schippel's *The History of the Production of Sugar*" (82). Among the soldiers, he is a "fiery agitator" for the Brest-Litovsk peace and gives a speech at the Congress of Eastern Peoples.

Novsky's texts provide the verbalization and articulation of his world (social injustice, human suffering, and lack of fulfillment), as well as its explanation (historical materialism), which is at the same time the assertion of this world's imminent revolutionary change. Living through these texts, Novsky takes the world as being completely known (as Hegel takes it) and interpreted. However, one should not stop at solely knowing the world. "The philosophers have only interpreted the world; the point, however, is to change it" (Marx's eleventh "Thesis on Feuerbach"). In other words, Novsky's texts interpret the world as a fully understood one that should now be changed.

The Hegelian "complete knowing" maintained in Boris Davidovich's texts of historical materialism sees each particular thing as the embodiment of a universal principle and thus intelligible by and through this principle. Boris Davidovich's "complete understanding" of the world is thus based on a concept of history as a rational totality rather than, for example, a series of free and contingent events. The events do not happen "by chance" but are brought about by an underlying principle. Idea is thus immanent to and identical with the world in all its particularities, and history is intelligible and readable in the light of its idea, its "real principle." In Hegel, the "inward" idea—as telos—is posed as already identical with the "outward" world, the identity being achieved in Hegel's philosophy itself. In Boris Davidovich Novsky's texts of historical materialism, this identity between the idea and the world, or between ratio and history, is to be achieved through the material practice of social revolution.

2. Negativity of the Antithesis

The first modus of Novsky's relating to the world is his being "through texts" that make the world fully understandable and known. But the texts that Novsky reads and listens to or writes and speaks do not exist as texts or language separated from material practice. Already at the age of thirteen, Boris Davidovich ceases to only read and listen to his texts: he starts to act according to them. "At thirteen, under the influence of Vladimir Soloviev's Antichrist, he ran away from home, but was brought back, escorted by police from a distant station." (76)

Novsky's response to his later texts of historical materialism is "not an analysis or interpretation of that what/how is said, but rather 'action.' The answer to these texts is in a sphere of immediacy; these texts and language continue in the practice," are an immanent aspect and part of material practice.[53] In other words, Novsky cannot remain only a reader or a writer of his texts: he has to respond to them by his material practice. Novsky's practice attempts to realize the texts of revolution, materialize the "goal of history" (a revolutionary overthrow of class society and its exploitation and alienation), and thus achieve the postulated identity between the idea of the world and the world.

Following his "theoretical" living through texts that interpret the world, the second modus of Novsky's practice is negativity, or the material destruction and breaking down of everything and everyone that stands in the way of the revolution as identity of the idea of the world (telos), on one hand, and the world, on the other. This material destruction gradually replaces Novsky's living through language. His organizing of the 1913 street demonstrations in St. Petersburg, where the physicality of the masses is still mitigated by the language of their demands and declarations, is followed by his joining a "terrorist group preparing for assassinations with bombs" (77), obviously without the usage of any accompanying texts. Novsky's ensuing material destruction includes "spectacular assassinations" (80) before the 1917 revolution, "terrifying explosions" against the enemies of the revolution after it happened (85), fighting for the new Soviet empire "against the rebellious and despotic emirs in Turkestan" (88) in 1920, the "liquidation of banditry in the Tambov region" (88) in 1921, and so on. The work of negativity takes place during the prerevolutionary period and the first few turbulent years after the revolution.

In the chronicle of Novsky, the action of destruction is presented as rushing without reflection, a practice in which Novsky only executes things he acknowledged to be necessary during his "theoretical" phase. In a letter to his fiancée, Zinaida Mihailovna Maysner, Novsky writes:

> During the brief periods of my freedom I watched, as in a movie theater, the passing of sad Russian villages, towns, people, and events, but I was always in flight—on a horse, on a boat, in a cart. . . . My only passion was this arduous, rapturous, and mysterious profession of revolutionary. . . . (85)

The dematerialization of reality "in a movie theater" resembles the dematerialization of reality in a work of negativity of the revolution. Reality is dematerialized (that is, "emptied of itself," so to speak) because it is regarded as only the means or obstacles of a sweeping ("I was always in flight") idealistic scheme. The world is a place for rewriting, in another medium, the idea of history, that is, the already written and finished texts of Novsky's "being through language." The world becomes dematerialized and devalued because it is seen as the "otherness" that has to be appropriated by and shaped according to the idea of the history enforced by the "idealistic" revolution.

3. Missing Synthesis

The work of negativity is gradually replaced by the third modus of Novsky's practice: the "positive" work of what was supposed to be the creation of a new and just society which would realize the utopia foreseen in the texts of Novsky's past "living through language." In this period, however, Novsky is described as having lost his "zeal" and having a "dull gaze" (88). "[I]n Kazakhstan, in the Central Office for Communications and Liaisons . . . he was bored" (89).

It is beyond the chronicle writer's domain to be able to say why Novsky lost his zeal and wore a "dull gaze." However, one can guess the obvious: the texts of Novsky's first modus of living through language—texts announcing a different, better world after the destruction of the old one—did not start getting realized.[54] On the contrary, these texts were lost through the practices of revolution, in general, including Novsky's practices, in particular. The final synthesis and goal of revolution is missing, receding farther and farther away in the utopian distance. The arrest and interrogation of Novsky, the main part of the story "A Tomb for Boris Davidovich," take place in the foreground of this absent synthesis.

The Anticlosure Practices of Absurdity

The story "A Tomb for Boris Davidovich" focuses on the interrogation of Boris Davidovich Novsky. At one point, the interrogator Fedukin's "intuitive genius" (94) manages to find a psychological device with which he breaks Novsky, who is now willing to admit that he is "guilty," that is, that he worked to sabotage the revolution. Both Boris Davidovich and Fedukin know and openly agree that this confession of "guilt" is completely fictional and has nothing to do with reality.

> Fedukin knew just as well as Novsky (and let him know it) that all this—the entire text of confession, formulated on ten closely typed pages—was pure fiction, which he alone, Fedukin, had concocted during the long hours of the night, typing with two fingers awkwardly and slowly (he liked to do everything himself). (98)

Both Novsky and Fedukin also know that the fact of Boris Davidovich's innocence is irrelevant. What matters is the text of his confession, the future sign of Boris Davidovich, since it is "probably the only document of his that would remain after his death" (98).

Boris Davidovich "fought with unsuspected strength for every word, every phrase" (98). Fighting for the text of his confession, Boris Davidovich returns to his first way of relating to the world, to his mode of being through texts and language that interpret the world and inform the material (revolutionary) practices that change it. But unlike before, Novsky now does not attempt to write the text that accepts the premises of his past readings, the postulates of historical materialism, and the inevitability of history and revolution. Fighting for his confession, Boris Davidovich now wants to write a different text that would convey to future generations some new and different knowledge from what Boris Davidovich himself grasped from his own past readings.

In the "only document of his that would remain after his death," Boris Davidovich tries to incorporate "a certain wording that would . . . whisper to a future investigator . . ." the distinctiveness of his new knowledge (98). Achieving their understanding of the world largely through texts (in the same way in which Boris Davidovich did it in his time), these new generations will have a chance to inform their own practice by reading Boris Davidovich Novsky's confession. And if they manage to decipher "contradictions and exaggerations" "skillfully woven" (98) by Novsky in his confession, then these future investigators would arrive at a very different interpretation of the world—and a very different material practice—from the one that marked Novsky's revolutionary life.

> Through long nights the two men [Novsky and Fedukin] struggled over the difficult text of the confession, panting and exhausted, their heads bent over the pages enveloped in the thick cigarette smoke, each trying to incorporate into it some of his own passion, his own beliefs, his own outlook from a higher perspective. (98)

Attempting to incorporate the "certain wording" that would convey his new knowledge to the future readers, Boris Davidovich has to struggle with the investigator Fedukin over the text of his confession. Each of the two men wants to shape Novsky's confession according to his own distinctive "beliefs" and "outlooks." Fedukin was "not interested in the so-called facts" but rather in "certain assumptions" (98).

> [I]t was better that the so-called truth of a single man . . . be destroyed than that higher . . . principles be questioned. . . . . . . What provoked Fedukin's fury and dedicated hatred was precisely this sentimental egocentricity of the accused, their pathological need to prove their own *innocence*, their own little *truths*, this neurotic going around in circles of so-called facts. . . . It enraged him that this blind truth of theirs could not be incorporated into a system of higher value. (99)

In order to preserve a system of "higher principles"—of the interpretation of the world and the respective material practice—Fedukin needs to destroy individual truths/facts "which could not be incorporated into a system . . . ." The Idea of the world, a guarantor of the rationality and justifiability of everything, is more important than the world itself and its "tiny organism(s)" (99) of individual people. The "so-called truths/facts" that cannot be incorporated in the system/Absolute Idea would prove the system wrong in its pretensions of absolute validity. Therefore, Fedukin needs to destroy these facts or, rather, shape them into the fitting elements of the absolute system. If Novsky is arrested, he must be guilty, so consequently he is guilty.

For his part, Novsky "rejected any assumption beforehand," and was trying to show that the "whole structure of this confession"—proving the validity of the system and the Absolute Idea—"rested on a lie . . ." (98). Novsky was trying to assert the fact and the truth of his innocence, which "could not be incorporated into the system." By doing so, Novsky was destroying the system itself.

In the battle for the text of Boris Davidovich's confession, Fedukin's side is one of the grand system (of "higher principles"), which claims to reveal the all-inclusive ratio of the world. Such a system proclaims that the numerous "little truths" that cannot be incorporated into it simply do not exist. In opposition to Fedukin, Boris Davidovich is struggling to preserve and articulate precisely these numerous "little truths," which, by their sheer existence, point at the invalidity of absolute systems. Thus, in his confession, Novsky tries to create a text that would go against the literature of historical materialism that he himself had read and created earlier. This literature asserted the system/idea of the whole, which fully explained every reality as the fitting element of this whole. The people's practice was consequently seen as simply an execution of the inevitable course of history, execution based on the "right" knowledge of what this course of history actually is.

If truths and facts cannot be incorporated into a system of higher principles, into a History that is identical to the Absolute Idea, then history is not a rational totality of a self-realizing idea/system and cannot be explained nor made according to that idea. Boris Davidovich wants to leave to "future investigators" his confession as the text that would communicate to them his newly acquired knowledge—his rejection of the concept of history as a rational totality that is fully understandable and fully understood.

The story "A Tomb for Boris Davidovich" displays the myth of absolute rationality as the core of the myth of revolution. While the myth of revolution might be more connected to Boris Davidovich's own times, its basis, the myth of absolute rationality and explicability of the world, is relevant and dangerous much beyond those times. This myth claims that the world is fully rational (understandable, explicable) and can thus be completely explained by an already achieved idea. This idea contains knowledge not only of the world's past and present but also of its future, which is yet to be realized. Thus, the idea's own realization through practice (which is fully determined by this idea) is equal to the world's own self-realization. In the myth of revolution, this idea of the world is entirely present as an idea—it has been completely thought out and verbalized—but is not yet present as material reality. The function of revolution is to entirely realize the idea of the world in the world in order for this world to come to its own self-fulfillment and telos.

As the particular version of the myth of absolute rationality, the myth of revolution is based on Hegel's and Marx's philosophies turned into or practiced as a myth. Philosophical thinking of absolute rationality becomes a mythic belief in absolute rationality and in the complete explicability of the past, present, and future. In the light of the Absolute Idea fully explaining the world, events do not happen "by chance" but are brought about by an underlying principle. The myth of absolute rationality becomes the basis of thinking and practicing the world, as well as the basis of an individual's own living. Thus, Boris Davidovich's biography displays the one embodiment of the dialectical principle present in Hegel and Marx: thesis (Novsky's living through texts that interpret the world) is followed by antithesis (Novsky's material practice of destruction of the existing world), and the (missing) synthesis. The three-step progress of Boris Davidovich's biography mirrors the larger three-step system of the idea of the whole world, the idea that sees itself as identical with the world.

The absence of a victorious synthesis of the revolutionary's biography (Novsky's boredom and arrest) mirroring the absence of a synthesis of the revolutionary's world destroys the whole system and the myth of absolute rationality. Boris Davidovich's confession attempts to articulate the world and practice in which truths and facts "cannot be incorporated into the system." This confession marks the second main stage of Kiš's dismantling of cultural closures—after articulating and opposing the closure of absolute irony by his creation of referentiality, Kiš now articulates and opposes the closure of absolute rationality by pointing at the need for a different way of thinking and practicing the world.

By opposing the Absolute Idea in his confession, Novsky tries to articulate the world in which things do not have to happen the way they do nor are they predetermined to happen that way. Dismantling the concept of history as an inevitable materialization of an absolute preexisting idea, Boris Davidovich tries to articulate history as something different, as a space in which one does not materialize preexisting ideas, but rather attempts to find a different way of practice and of thinking. This different way might be the one in which, if history is not the idea's self-identity, then contingencies or potential openings, places of indeterminacy, should not be rationalized away. Such a history requires knowledges and practices that are different from both absolute irony, on one hand, and identity between the idea and the world (or the myth of absolute rationality), on the other.

The world and history that Boris Davidovich wants to articulate in his confession is the world of facts and truths that "cannot be incorporated into a system" and do not constitute or spell out a system—a world of contingencies or "absurdity." In "the final page of [his] autobiography which he had been consciously writing with his blood and brains for some forty years," in "the sum of his living" (92), Boris Davidovich is trying to communicate to future readers the existence and importance of contingencies. His "last testament" (92) thus carries an opening, a challenge and a question to future generations: how can the "absurd" world, the world that we cannot fully "know" because preconceived ideas are not completely identical with it, be known and practiced?

If absurdity is seen not as a negative closure but as a positive opening, one can see that the "absurd" world rejects both the endless evasiveness of absolute irony and the final solution of the "absolute truth" (such as Fedukin's) in favor of constant readjustments and remakings of the contingent truths. In a history that is not "fully known" as a self-identity of the idea (final synthesis), preconceived ideas do not get materialized through material practice—at all costs of the "so-called individual truths"—but rather changed. Thus, "error is . . . a failure to adjust immediately from a preconception to an actuality" (Cage, *Silence*, 170–71). In other words, ideas are not realized through material practice but rather continually created and re-created through it. The practices of knowing and doing become the practices of idea's alteration rather than identity.

How can one think and practice such a world and history? In *Silence*, John Cage explores this question. He is the "future investigator" of Boris Davidovich Novsky's words who gets Novsky's message and attempts to respond to it.

Danilo Kiš opposes the closure of language irony by creating referentiality of the word "revolutionary." At the end of Kiš's search for the referentiality of this word and for the missing history, Boris Davidovich Novsky's confession articulates as closure the myth of the fully known (and completely determinate) world of the idea's self-identity. If the world is not to be seen as already fully known, then the thinking of a potentially liberating opposition needs to be more "elastic," changing its ideas so fast as not to repeat the error of failing to "adjust immediately from a preconception / to an actuality."

The closure of the myth of the fully known world in Boris Davidovich's confession is identical to the closure of the idealist construction of language and material practice articulated in Cage's work. Boris Davidovich's confession, as the end of Kiš's search for the referentiality of the word "revolutionary," thus articulates as a closure the same thing as Cage's writings: the idealist "vertical" ("Platonic") construction of both language terms and corresponding material (social) practices according to the pregiven ideas of what they should be. The following discussion will show how Cage's *Silence* articulates a liberating language that is not idealistic but "materialistic."

Silence

The Closure of "Vertical" Construction of Language Terms and the Shaping of Ideas by Power Centers

No one can have an idea

30"

once he starts really listening.
(*Silence*, 191)

> **Another way of**
> . . . .
> saying it is: "Do not be
> . . . .
> satisfied with approximations
> . . . .
> (or just: Do not be satisfied) but insist
> . . . .
> (as you need not) on what comes
> . . . .
> to you."
>
> (257–58)

"Vertical" construction of language terms, which Cage opposes, is referred to in many texts. A simple example of "vertical" construction can be seen in the definition of the term "music" from various texts in *Silence*. In "The Future of Music: Credo," the term "music" is constructed "vertically" in relation to the already given ideas of what "music" is: "musical sounds," "harmony," "18th and 19th century instruments." In "Experimental Music," the same term is "vertically" constructed in relation to the notions of "being connected with the composer's memory and imagination," and in "Experimental Music: Doctrine," in relation to the ideas of "psychology," "theme," and "purpose." In "Indeterminacy" (part 2 of "Composition as Process"), the term is vertically constructed according to the idea of "composition being determinate with respect to its performance," and so on.

"Vertical" construction of language terms is the construction of terms and the corresponding material practice in relation to already given ideas of what these terms are about. This "vertical" construction is a closure because it does not allow for the redefinition of terms and the change of practice. This closure also enables the social relations of domination because the nonmaterial fixed ideals, which are asserted in their primacy over potentially liberating material practice, are shaped by power centers.

For example, terms such as "music," "art," "lecture," "language," "text," "meaningful life," and so on define themselves "vertically," in relation to already given notions of what "music" or "art" is. These given notions are not unequivocally communal; they are to a large extent "forced" upon and inscribed within the community by established power centers. Constructing oneself in relation to these ideas is thus directly connected to social subservience.

Centers of power establish the specific constructions of terms such as, for example, "nonmusical field of sound," "music," and "painting." The nonmusical field of sound is defined by, among other centers, academia as being "academically forbidden" (5). The makers of electronic musical instruments (like the Theremin company) construct "music" as sounds produced by only traditionally "musical" instruments: "Thereministes act as censors. . . . We are shielded from new sound experiences" (4). The characteristics that define painting or art in general are created by "someone [who] arranged [that we] should" (100) recognize certain objects and activities as art.

The "vertical" construction of language and practice or attempting "to follow in someone's footsteps" is "what we're taught to do" (214). The terms of everyday language and practice constitute themselves through an *approximation* ("the closer the better") of the ideal forms given by the power centers. The subjects are constructed as already defined by the given (external) notions of what they are and are always inherently lacking in relation to these notions of what they "should" be.

Cage is not interested in exploring the "attraction" of the establishment's vertical structures. It is important, however, to point out that the aura of these power centers comes from their self-presentation as "community" instances. Being in them (by them) means being seen and heard by many, "accepted" by many, and thus "really" (socially, politically) living. If the sense of ourselves comes from the others' sense of ourselves, a sense of being from the others' acknowledgment that we "are," then the self-representation of the centers of power as the community gives them the decisive importance for our self-constructing of ourselves.

Language terms and forms of practice define themselves in relation to the centers of power. One's becoming "someone" is defined by these centers. "To be" means to become something else, "the other" of oneself, the external center. Thus, one loses all the potential ways of being without regard to this center, all the not-yet-existent "oneselves."

The Closure of Self-Expression

22'00"
What I think & what I feel can be
my inspiration but it is then also my
pair of blinders. To see one must go
beyond the imagination and for that
one must stand absolutely still as though
10" in the center of a leap.
. . . .
every me out of the way. An error is simply a
23'00" failure to adjust immediately from a preconception
to an actuality.

(170–71)

Although self-expression may construct itself against the world, as the negation of the present state and an announcement of the potential utopian not-yet-being, this self-expression as the realization of subjectivity is not the oppositional answer to the vertical construction of language and material practice according to the external power centers. On the contrary, the "vertical" closure-producing constructions include the construction of language and practice as "self-expression." Language as self-expression is constructed in relation to the given "inner" centers of subjectivity and/or to the subjective preconceptions of how the world should be.

Although many of Cage's works express his thoughts on "what should be done" to "improve the world," his utopian vision does not see freedom as literal self-expression, that is, as our ability to "shape" the environment and to make the world "our own" in the sense of direct material realization of our preconceptions or subjectivity.

> How can I get it to come to me of itself, not just pop up out of my
>   memory, taste, and psychology?
> How?
> Do you know how?
>
> (48)

In the frame of self-expression, language is constructed "vertically" in relation to subjectivity or preconceptions, which, once articulated, attempt to realize themselves in material practice and make the world according to one's own image. The other(s) become the obstacles to my freedom.

For Cage, freedom is not a materialization of our preconceived ideas or of our subjectivity, or the shaping of world as self-expression. Language should not be constructed vertically as the expression of ideas and forms according to which reality is to be shaped. The whole structure by which language as self-expression articulates reality as it "should be" and by which reality is always already deficient in regard to the ideas of its perfection is "intolerable." This structure is intolerable not because the world is perfect but because the material (social) practice is regarded as an imperfect mimesis of thought and not as a not-yet-known reality in itself.

Practice is constructed as the mimetic repetition of thought, and language is constructed as the expression of thought that leads to this thought's material realization. Language is determined by thought, and, in its turn, language determines the practice. Both language and practice are limited by this structure.

"If I have a particular purpose, and then a series of actions comes about, and all I get is an approximation of my purpose, then nothing but a sort of compromise or disappointment can take place."[55] Compromise, disappointment, and pale approximation, on one hand, and the "subservience" and control of material reality according to our ideas, on the other hand: this is an "intolerable situation." At the same time subjects and objects of material practices, we are disappointed as subjects and controlled as objects. Language as the self-expression of preconceptions or subjectivity that wants to be realized, as the blueprint for reality, is language constructed within and by these closures.

Self-expression leads to the control of practice according to one's already existing notions. The control of one's linguistic and material practice according to one's notions does not allow the possibility of being a subject because the forms of practice are limited by one's notions of this practice:

> Their ears are walled in
> with sounds
> 10" of their own imagination.
> (155)

In other words, trying to materialize one's notions of what one should be, one subordinates one's material practice to these notions, and thus one does not allow the creation and exploration of material practices' "own ways of being." The control of practice by the "walls of one's own imagination" is the objectification of this practice and of one's material being.

> without intention? Do not memory, psychology—
> ANSWER: "—never again." (17)

Horizontal Interaction among a Plurality of Centers

Cage articulates and subverts the "vertical" construction of language as the closure of language by reacting to it. (Literature reacts to the situation it "brought into being" in the first place.) His method is not negative, saying what it is that he is against, but rather positive, creating instances of anticlosure practices. Vertical construction should be "silenced" so that other ways of being can be attempted: "nothing was lost when everything was given away. In fact, everything is gained" (8).

The language and material (artistic and social) practice should not be constructed vertically, in relation to one given external center, but rather horizontally, through interaction among a plurality of centers.

> IN ALL OF SPACE EACH THING AND
> EACH HUMAN BEING IS AT THE CENTER . . . EACH
> ONE . . .   IS THE MOST HONORED
> ONE OF ALL.   INTERPENETRATION [WITH AND] . . .
> . . . .

. . .
BY EVERY OTHER ONE . . .

. . . .
EACH AND EVERY THING . . . IS RELATED TO
EACH AND EVERY OTHER THING . . .

(46–47)

all things . . . *are* related, and . . . this complexity is more evident when it is not oversimplified by an idea of relationship in one person's mind. (260)

It is thus possible to make a musical composition the continuity of which is free of individual taste and memory (psychology) and also of the literature and "traditions" of the art. The sounds enter the time-space centered within themselves, unimpeded by service to any abstraction, their 360 degrees of circumference free for an infinite play of interpenetration. (59)

Each thing that is there is a subject. It is a situation involving multiplicity. (101)

Activities . . .

. . . .
are each central, original.

(97)

In the anarchically dehierarchized horizontal plane, liberated from the always already made definitions of a high center, one can attempt to become oneself by interacting with others rather than by approximating the given notions of being asserted by power centers. "Horizontal" interaction among a plurality of centers is in Cage's work defined as nonobstruction among the centers ("a non-obstruction of sounds is of the essence"[39]) and the absence of fusion ("no harmonious fusion of sound is essential" [39]). The centers are in a state of interpenetration.

INTERPENETRATION MEANS THAT EACH ONE OF THESE MOST HONORED ONES OF ALL IS MOVING OUT IN ALL DIRECTIONS PENETRATING AND BEING PENETRATED BY EVERY OTHER ONE NO MATTER WHAT THE TIME OR WHAT THE SPACE.   SO THAT WHEN ONE SAYS THAT THERE IS NO CAUSE AND EFFECT, WHAT IS MEANT IS THAT THERE ARE AN INCALCULABLE INFINITY OF CAUSES AND EFFECTS, THAT IN FACT EACH AND EVERY THING IN ALL OF TIME AND SPACE IS RELATED TO EACH AND EVERY OTHER THING IN ALL OF TIME AND SPACE.

(46–47)

Cage's text "2 Pages, 122 Words on Music and Dance" (96; see also page 61 of this book) is a graphic example of "horizontal" interaction among a plurality of centers. The lines or groupings of text (one word, one sentence, or irregular stance) are scattered on the paper, without diachronic relation. There is no fusion, and no "integration of the individual in the group" (5) happens. Every instance of text is separated from every other one by an empty space of white paper. The empty spaces allow for the nonobstruction of the centers.

The white paper functions as a background that asserts the synchronical presence of everything on it. The shortness of the piece and its visual realization allow for the simultaneous presence of all its "centers." Each center has a space for its own concentric circles of sound and meaning, like a stone thrown into the water, the ever-new outer circles of one center interpenetrating with the outer circles of other centers.

In most of the texts in *Silence*, the forms that Cage uses assert the space and time for each of the given centers of the text, allowing them to interpenetrate with other centers without being obstructed.

In "Lecture on Nothing," for example, "there are four measures in each line and twelve lines in each unit of the rhythmic structure. There are forty-eight such units, each having forty-eight measures. The whole is divided into five large parts, in the proportion 7, 6, 14, 14, 7. The forty-eight measures of each unit are likewise so divided . . ." (109). This rhythmical structure creates units of text on a few different levels: five large parts, or forty-eight units of twelve lines, or 576 lines, or 2,304 smallest rhythmical measures of text or silence. None of these levels is asserted as the dominant or primary one, the realization of which would be the goal of other levels. The smallest rhythmical measures, for example, are not obstructed as individual centers by their creation of sentences and "speech." On this level, the "empty" spaces between the units of texts and the units of texts between the "empty" spaces (or between the "empty" times in the performance of the piece) assert the centrality of each of these smallest rhythmical measures.

Each moment   is absolute,   alive and significant.   Blackbirds   rise   from a field making   a

(113)

In "Where Are We Going? and What Are We Doing?" the printed text attempts to mimic the performance in which four lectures read by a single lecturer are heard simultaneously. The four lectures are printed in four different fonts. The four first lines of the four texts are printed one under another, then there is empty space, then the four second lines of the four texts are printed one under another, and so on.

The asserted and nonobstructed centers are the lines of the texts and the empty spaces that take place in the absence of the text and in between the groups of four lines. The lines of one text are separated from other lines of the same text in such a way that an automatic "fusion" of these lines in the production of a meaning of the text is impossible. The nonobstructed centers interpenetrate with each other and the reader. Various interactions among the centers and a reader are possible. One could try to create, for example, the first lecture by following every first line of the four-line stanzas, or one could read four lines of each stanza one after another, and so on.

Communication and Interpenetration

A "false" community creates itself through a few "elevated" centers, such as media or institutions. Communication within the community is in many ways reduced to communication via and through these centers. Communication with others in the community is seen as possible only via these centers. One thinks that only if one achieves the position in any pregiven center, one can communicate with the others.

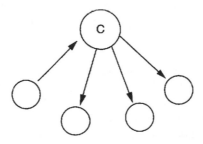

However, as (Cage's) Marshall McLuhan warns, the media is the message, and the center shapes us and determines our language. Going through the center, we become more the center and less ourselves.

In Cage's horizontal plurality of centers, alternative communication is made possible by developed technology. At present, technology is used in existing social formations (capitalism, "mass culture") for particular power goals. However, Cage's point is that this same technology could be used as a means for horizontal communication in which everyone could directly communicate with everyone else, without the use of an "intermediary" or external center.

EACH AND EVERY THING IN ALL OF TIME AND SPACE IS RELATED TO EACH AND EVERY OTHER THING IN ALL OF TIME AND SPACE.

(47)

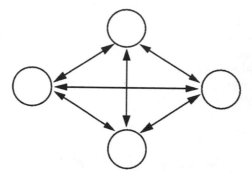

"Horizontal" being is being in which one does not define oneself and one's language vertically, according to the given centers of power, meaning, or subjectivity. "Horizontal" being is being of potential freedom: trying to become oneself through interactions with others and not through approximation of the already given center. The subject is not constituted through the complete control of one's material (linguistic and social) practice by one's ideas because this control limits and objectifies one's practice. The subject is constituted through explorations of the possibilities of freedom outside of the realm of one's control and preconceptions, as "a leap out of the reach of one's own grasp of oneself" (162). This freedom does not turn others into passive objects but rather presupposes their active agency.

For example, in the aforementioned "2 Pages, 122 Words on Music and Dance," the number of words in the text, as well as the position on paper of the fragments of text, was not determined by the subject (author) but by "chance operations" and "imperfections in the sheets of paper" (96). Thus, the subject (as the author) himself is constituted through freedom, which is not his own control of everything he could control but rather his interaction with other centers (paper, chance operations).

Liberated "horizontal" being is not that of complete control of oneself and others (of "environment") but that of the "interpenetration" and the awareness of this interpenetration among a multiplicity of centers. "Each thing that is there is a subject. It is a situation involving multiplicity" (101). This "interpenetration" produces "chance" situations, which are not controlled by any one of the centers but are rather brought about by their interaction.

For example, in the performance of "Where Are We Going? and What Are We Doing?" the four centers of the four simultaneously given lectures interact with the numerous centers of the individuals in the audience. Moving in the space or focusing on one lecture (attempting to get the "meanings"), or listening to all of the lectures together (getting sounds), or doing something else, every center of the audience interacts in different ways with the other centers of the audience and with the four centers of the performance. The interactions, though, not only are contingent upon the audience but are also shaped by the centers of the performance—by their loudness, sound, by how long they have been "turned on," and so on. What happens is chance interpenetration among a multitude of centers.

Liberating Self-Alteration

Chance situations created in interpenetration of the multitude of centers open the possibility of being as self-alteration. Freedom is not self-expression but rather self-alteration. "It is by reason of this fact that we are made perfect by what happens to us rather than by what we do" (64). Others are not the obstacle of my freedom but the condition of it.

And then when we actually	Go back to the beginning and
. . . .	. . . .
set to work, a kind of	change everything? Or do
. . . .	. . . .
avalanche came about which	we continue and give up
. . . .	. . . .
corresponded not at all	what had seemed to be
. . . .	. . . .
with that beauty which had	where we were going? Well,
. . . .	. . . .
seemed to appear to us as an	what we do is go straight
. . . .	. . . .
objective. Where do we go	on; that way lies, no doubt,
. . . .	. . . .
then? Do we turn around?	a revelation. I had no idea. . . .
. . . .	(221–22)

Is when Rauschenberg looks an idea? Rather it is an entertainment in which to celebrate unfixity. (98)

			He has changed
the responsibility of	the composer	from making	to accepting
			(129)

Cage's anecdotes often narrate cases of unpredicted interactions that bring different kinds of self-alterations. One of the clearest cases of self-alteration is the one at the end of Cage's story about his apprenticeship for the architect Goldfinger in Paris:

> After a month of working with Goldfinger, measuring the dimensions of rooms which he was to modernize, answering the telephone, and drawing Greek columns, I overheard Goldfinger saying, "To be an architect, one must devote one's life solely to architecture." I then left him, for, as I explained, there were other things that interested me, music and painting for instance. (261)

Some other stories narrate instances of real-life estrangement. Created by chance interactions, these estrangements point at the untold but implicated and potential self-alteration of the ways in which the stories' characters and readers perceive the specific events or use the language.

> Merce Cunningham's father delights in gardening. Each year he has had to move the shrubs back from the driveway to protect them from being run over when Mrs. Cunningham backs out. One day Mrs. Cunningham in backing out knocked down but did not hurt an elderly gentleman who had been taking a stroll. Getting out of her car and seeing him lying on the sidewalk, Mrs. Cunningham said, "What are you doing there?" (272)

> Then we had to go back to New Haven to do the TV class over again. This time on the way back it was a very hot and humid day. We stopped again in Newtown, but at a different place, for some ice. There was a choice: raspberry, grape, lemon, orange, and pineapple. I took grape. It was refreshing. I asked the lady who served it whether she had made it. She said, "Yes." I said, "Is it fresh fruit?" She said, "It's not fresh, but it's fruit." (268)

When Cage writes "we are converted to the enjoyment of our possessions from wanting what we don't have" (103), he does not mean that everything is just great as it is and we should stop criticizing it and start enjoying it. Rather, he means that we should first stop being fixed on the few vertical centers and their proclamations of what we should want but can never have. "Enjoyment of our possessions," then, means exploring the nonmaterialized potential of "horizontal" being; it means becoming aware of the multiplicity of centers, of the "centrality" of each one of them, and of "chance" interpenetration among them. The freedom in chance interpenetration is not one achieved by the practice of self-expression as control of the objects but rather one of practice as self-alteration (but never fusion or obstruction) of the being as "connectedness" with the others. This freedom is (could be) in "our possession" and should be "enjoyed."

For the field is not a field	*of human awareness, and the*
. . . .	. . . .
of music, and the acceptance is	*acceptance ultimately is*
. . . .	. . . .
not just of the sounds that	*of oneself as present mysterious-*
. . . .	. . . .
had been considered useless, ugly,	*ly, impermanently, on*
. . . .	. . . .
and wrong, but it is a field	*this limitless occasion.*
. . . .	(215–16)

water is fine.   Jump in.   Some will refuse,   for they see that the
water is thick with   monsters   ready to devour them.   What they have   in
mind   is self-preservation.   And what is that   self-preservation but
only a preservation   from life?   Whereas life without death is no longer life   but
only self-preservation.

(134)

The Creation of Language through Material Practice

Cage's own explorations of liberated "horizontal" being, interpenetrations of multiple centers, and the role of chance in these interpenetrations can be more easily
seen in his performances or in the reconstruction of many texts from *Silence* as
performances than in the reading of the texts from *Silence* as texts. A performance
allows the synchronicity of events that graphically shows the horizontal being of
multiple centers, while the text creates the diachrony that makes seeing of this
horizontal interpenetration more difficult.[56]

However, while synchronicity allows a more graphical "display" of horizontal
interactions, the important point is that synchronicity is not a precondition or
aspect of horizontal interaction among the plurality of centers.

> Activities which are different
> happen in a time which is a space:
> are each central, original.
>
> (97)

"Time is a space." This concept is often taken as a concept of time of repetitive
commodity production, devoid of historicity and change. For Cage, though, time
as a space is a concept that enables the horizontal interaction of all the multiple
centers. In one space, all the centers exist simultaneously and horizontally. These

centers are not negated as only a means of the progression through time of the grand scheme, telos, end, and purpose of the whole interaction. Time as a space, or horizontal interaction of multiple centers, asserts the multifaceted "fullness" of each center and opposes the transformation of this fullness into the homogenizing and one-dimensional level of "one moment" in the progress of history or in development of "subjectivity," "tradition," and so on.

If one reconstructs Cage's texts as performances, the textual part of these performances becomes only one of a few horizontally related centers. The other centers are music, gestures, dance, loudness of voice, performers, units of time, and so on. The textual parts, or the language of these performances, are constituted (in some aspects) through interaction with other centers. In "Changes," for example, the first part of the "Composition as Process," interactions between author and chance operations determine the lengths of units of (given) speech and music: "[I]nterruptions of the speech [when music is played] like the lengths of the paragraphs themselves, were the result of chance operations" (18).

In the performance (specific reading or printing) of "On Robert Rauschenberg, Artist, and His Work," it is the reader or printer who determines the form in which the text appears in that particular reading or printing, given that the text "may be read in whole or in part; any sections of it may be skipped, what remains may be read in any order. . . . Any of the sections may be printed directly over any of the others, and the spaces between the paragraphs may be varied in any manner" (98).

In this case, one does not deal with the one text, given that different inter-actions, that is, different *"final" texts,* are possible among the centers of readers or printers and the centers of Cage's text.

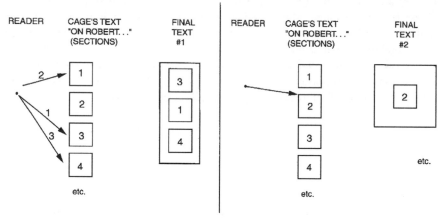

In the performance of "Robert Rauschenberg . . . ," Cage's text is a multiplicity of given centers that horizontally interrelate with another center, that of a reader or a printer. The "final" text of each performance is created through this interaction ("interpenetration"). That "final" text *is* this unique interpenetration. Thus, language is not constructed as the "expression" of vertical centers (ideas) that get materialized in practice (which itself gets to be the mimesis of the mimesis). Rather, language is constituted *through* the material practice: "It is not a question of going in to oneself or out to the world. It is rather a condition of fluency that's in and out" (161).

In the creation of language through material practice, chance operations function as the (limited) negations of the vertical ideal center (idea of what the text should be like), which would otherwise fully determine the text. In other words, chance functions as the mimicking of the "organic" (nonmechanistic and unpredictable) activity and interpenetration of the centers themselves.

Questions, Cold Ashes, Silence

Some of the ways in which language is constituted in the interaction with other centers, that is, through material practice, are (1) language and texts as questions; (2) language as transient thought that should be "dropped as . . . cold ashes of a fire long dead" (39); and (3) language as silence.

Questions

Speaking about his compositions, Cage says:

> Instead of representing my control, they represent questions that I've asked and the answers that have been given by means of chance operations. I've merely changed my responsibility from making choices to asking questions. It's not easy to ask questions.[57]

Language formulates not the ideas that reality should follow but the questions to which material practice—a performance and/or practice of writing and speaking—gives the answers. What happens if we do the performance according to the particular "question"? How does it look? How does it sound? What happens if I write and read the text according to a particular time frame or a particular form? How does it look on the page? How does it sound when it is performed? It is not better or worse than I thought it would be, because I did not envision how and what it should be. "There are no mistakes, for once something happens it authentically is." "Music is simply trying things out in / school fashion to see what happens" (189). "No one can have an idea / once he starts really listening" (191).

"I write / in order to hear; never do I hear and / then write what I hear" (169): writing in order to hear and not hearing and then writing what one hears. Language is the questioning we do in order to find out the answers, and not the repetition of that which we "already know," or vertical construction of language according to pregiven ideas. The relation between language and material practice is not that between a blueprint and an execution of it but that between questions and answers: "[T]he action was a non-knowledge of something that had not yet happened" (39).

Language of questions is language of self-alteration through the interaction with material practices. This is not a limited "closed" language of self-expression but a language of creating oneself through self-alteration. One creates oneself not in relation to the past, as achieving something one already knows, but rather in relation to the present unrepeatable contingencies. One does not know what one is, because one is only in interaction with others and thus unpredictable and new to oneself. The practice, the gnoseological activity produced in this practice, and the language that allows it become open and unlimited. Others are not obstacles to one's freedom but the realization and condition of one's freedom and one's language.

Cold Ashes

> Thoughts arise not to be collected and cherished but to be dropped as though they were void. Thoughts arise not to be collected and cherished but to be dropped as though they were rotten wood. Thoughts arise not to be collected and cherished but to be dropped as though they were pieces of stone. Thoughts arise not to be collected and cherished but to be dropped as though they were the cold ashes of a fire long dead. (Meister Eckhart, quoted in *Silence*, 39)

The purpose of thoughts is not their preservation and hypostatization to the level of ideas. They arise in order to disappear, and their being is in their passing away. The instantaneous language that Cage marks, paralleling the instantaneousness of thoughts in Meister Eckhart's concept, is the language created horizontally, in the present moment, in the interaction with all the other centers. This language does not secure itself "in the thingness of a work" but rather marks and produces "instantaneous ecstasy" (65).

Attempting to dismantle the closures of vertical construction of language, Cage invites us to see and create the language of the present, the instantaneous language that constructs itself in relation to other centers. This language appears in and through specific interactions with the others, and it disappears at the moment when these specific interpenetrations with other centers are no more.

that our delight

lies in not   pos-sessing anything   .   Each moment

presents what happens   .

(111)

No-continuity
simply means   accepting that   continuity   that happens.
Continuity   means the opposite: making that particular continuity   that
excludes   all others.

(132)

Silence

Language of self-alteration is the language of full awareness of the others, of the "noise" that fills the silence of our projects, preconceptions, history, subjectivity, and so on. The language of silence is one that knows how to listen when the other centers (thus audible and present) act, so that it can construct itself as a reaction to the others, and not as (only) a self-determined action of its own talking.

It is not	just static: it is a quiet
. . . .	. . . .
in the nature of doing to	readiness for whatever and
. . . .	. . . .
improve but rather to come	the multiplicities are already
. . . .	. . . .
into being, to continue, to	there in the making. We watch
. . . .	. . . .
go out of being and to	for signs and accept omens.
. . . .	. . . .
be still, not doing. That	Everything is an omen, so
. . . .	. . . .
still not-doing is a	we continue doing and changing.
. . . .	
preparation. It is not	(235–36)
. . . .	

The Language of Community

Going against the closures of the "vertical" constructing of language according to pregiven "centers," Cage attempts to mark the liberating practices of language, which constructs itself through and by present material practice, practice of poetry and performance that is at the same time "a highly simplified" social practice. "Music is an oversimplification of the situation we actually are in" (149). This is self-altering and not "self-realizing" language, and it allows for the self-alteration, rather than self-expression, of a subject. Self-alteration permits the practice in which the others are not obstacles, but rather a condition of one's freedom.

Self-altering subject and language allow the creation of forms of reality that cannot be predicted or constructed by the already established "centers." New reality comes into being if language as (self-)expression of vertical ideas is "bracketed" away.

These new realities do not get created according to pregiven ideal texts (ideas, centers), but through the interaction among a just established, and already passing, multitude of centers. Language of this interaction is not the pregiven language of pregiven ideas that should be realized by practice but rather the language that gets created through this material practice.

This language is the language of community because it enables the creation of community not according to some external centers but according to or through the community's own practices of interaction ("interpenetration") among its numerous nonfixed centers. The creation of community is creation through self-alteration, not self-expression. Such a creation of community needs a "change of our minds" and of our language. In his work, Cage attempts to mark this "new" language of horizontal, material, and democratic—rather than vertical, ideal, and hierarchical—construction.

Through its liberating effects, a literary work at the same time indirectly articulates that which it liberates us from. Cage articulates the closures of "dictatorial" vertical structures (idea—language—practice, or composer—conductor—musicians) by reacting to them. In his reaction, Cage creates a liberating horizontal language and being characterized by practices of democratic interaction among a multiplicity of centers. By so doing, he offers an answer to the question of Danilo Kiš on the possible break from closures of both idealistic language and idealistic historical practice, a question that the revolutionary Boris Davidovich tried to "whisper to a future investigator" (*Tomb*, 98).[58]

A lady	from Texas	said:	I live in Texas	.
	We have no music	in Texas.		The reason they've no
music in Texas		is because		they have recordings
in Texas.	Remove the records from Texas			
	and someone	will learn to sing		.
	Everybody	has a song		
	which is	no	song at all :	
	it is a process	of singing		,
	and when you sing		,	
	you are	where you are		.

(126)

This piece appeared in Dance Magazine, November 1957. The two pages were given me in dummy form by the editors. The number of words was given by chance operations. Imperfections in the sheets of paper upon which I worked gave the position in space of the fragments of text. That position is different in this printing, for it is the result of working on two other sheets of paper, of another size and having their own differently placed imperfections.

2 Pages, 122 Words on Music and Dance

movement

sound

Activities which are different
happen in a time which is a space:
are each central, original.

The telephone rings.

Each person is in the best seat.

War begins at any moment.

are in the audience.

love
mirth
the heroic
wonder
tranquility
fear
anger
sorrow
disgust

Points in
time, in
space

The emotions

Is there a glass of water?

Each now is the time, the space.

lights

inaction?

Are eyes open?

Where the bird flies, fly.   ears?

To obtain the value
of a sound, a movement,
measure from zero. (Pay
attention to what it is,
just as it is.)

A bird flies.

Slavery is abolished.

the woods

A sound has no legs to stand on.

The world is teeming: anything can
happen.

John Cage, "2 Pages, 122 Words on Music and Dance" (*Silence*, 96–97)

Literature against the Closures of Power: This Way for the Gas, Ladies and Gentlemen by Tadeusz Borowski and The Remains of the Day by Kazuo Ishiguro

> "It's a great privilege, after all, to have been given a part to play, however small, on the world's stage."
>
> —Kazuo Ishiguro, The Remains of the Day

In this chapter, the concentration camp stories in This Way for the Gas, Ladies and Gentlemen (1976; Polish editions, 1948), by Polish writer Tadeusz Borowski, enter into a dialogue with British writer Kazuo Ishiguro's novel The Remains of the Day (1989). Ishiguro's novel is a first-person narrative of the impeccable English butler Stevens, who reminisces in the postwar period about his prewar actions, which, although allegedly with the best intentions, have actually abetted Nazi policies in inter bellum Britain. A dialogue between Borowski's stories and Ishiguro's novel reveals disturbing similarities between the seemingly different worlds depicted in these two literary works and shows the closures of power that the two works articulate through a liberating reaction to them.

Biographical Outlines

Tadeusz Borowski

Tadeusz Borowski, best known for his stories recounting years as an inmate of Auschwitz and Dachau, was born into a Polish family living in the Soviet Ukraine in 1922. Both his parents were sent to Soviet prison camps during his childhood. When Tadeusz was three years old,

> [b]ecause he once belonged to the Polish Military Organization, his father has been carted off to build what was probably the first *stroyka* of socialism, the White Sea Canal. . . . Before Tadeusz's eighth birthday, Teofila [Tadeusz's mother] was transported to Yenisei as a *chlyen syemi* (family member) of Stanislav Borowski. . . . Tadeusz was sent to a *dietdom* (children's home). They took away his house and they took away his school, where Tadeusz had already begun to learn Polish. An aunt from a nearby town . . . took him in. In the school in that town they spoke in [the Russian] language.[1]

Borowski's family reunited in Warsaw in 1934; Tadeusz, however, did not live at home but in a Franciscan boarding school. In 1939 Poland disappeared from the political map of the "New Europe" as Germany occupied it from the west and the Soviet Union from the east. Higher education was forbidden for Poles, but Borowski studied literature in underground classes and had his first book of poems—*Wherever the Earth*—published by an underground press. He was arrested by the Nazis in February 1943, as was his fiancée and a colleague from literature class, Maria Rundo.

Both Tadeusz and Maria were interrogated at Pawiak prison (where Borowski watched the Warsaw Ghetto Uprising) and sent to Auschwitz. Since April 1943, Borowski was an inmate first at Auschwitz and later at Dachau, until the liberation by the American army on May 1, 1945. The final part of Borowski's imprisonment was the worst:

> [F]or the first time . . . Borowski became a "Muslim" [someone who lost the will to live]. . . . [A]t the time of liberation Borowski did not weigh much more than 35 kg and could not get on his feet.[2]

From May 1945 until May 1946, Borowski lived in an American camp near Munich, then in Munich proper. He lost track of his fiancée and only in December of 1945 learned that she was in Sweden. The two lovers reunited in 1946 in Warsaw and got married. Considered to be one of the most promising young Polish writers on account of his concentration camp stories, which were published in 1946 (a collaboration with two friends) and 1948 (written by him alone), Tadeusz joined the Polish Communist Party and started writing mainly politically engaging articles. "I stepped on the throat of [my] own song," he allegedly said.[3] A few days after his wife bore a daughter, Borowski, in his third attempt at suicide, opened a gas valve in his apartment. He died on July 3, 1951, at twenty-eight years of age.

> Borowski . . . offered his talent to those who prided themselves on building the society he dreamed about in Auschwitz. His services were greatly appreciated and he became one of the most prominent writers in Stalinist Poland. . . . [A]t the beginning he had no doubts that he was fighting for a just cause. The truth revealed itself gradually. By the late 1940s it was clear to him that the Soviet civilization, which had liberated the concentration camps in Germany, relied on similar forms of oppression at home. This bitter discovery, as well as the sense that he had been caught up a second time in a vicious circle of suffering and oppression, were presumably the critical facts in his decision to commit suicide.[4]

Kazuo Ishiguro

Kazuo Ishiguro was born in Nagasaki, Japan, in 1954 and as a child moved with his parents to Great Britain. He was educated there, studying philosophy and English at Kent University and obtaining a master's degree in creative writing from the University of East Anglia. Ishiguro later worked for an independent welfare organization concerned with the homeless and unemployed. Much has been made of his Japanese origin and the fact that his first two novels take place in Japan; Ishiguro himself, however, repeatedly emphasizes that he actually knows very little about Japan and its culture, that his Japanese language skill is that of a five-year-old, and that his Japan is a place he invented in a certain way in order for his stories to work.[5] He is an unusually successful writer, has been awarded prestigious prizes for each of his first three novels,[6] and is openly pleased with his writing career and success. Turning down offers from journals, Ishiguro dedicates himself full-time to his writing. He now lives in London with his wife and daughter.

Looking in the Mirror, a Perfect English Butler Stevens Sees, as His Own Reflection, an Auschwitz Inmate

What is the connection between the writings of the tragic Polish writer Tadeusz Borowski and those of successful contemporary British writer Kazuo Ishiguro? Both authors write about World War II. Located in the center of horror and death, the concentration camp, the narrator of Borowski's stories recounts the violence that he witnessed and committed himself. He makes disturbing discoveries about the nature of victimization and survival, discoveries as pertinent for times of peace as they were during the war. The novels of Kazuo Ishiguro, on the other hand, never take the war as their direct subject, but they focus on the individuals whose lives are irretrievably marked by their participation in the making of the war or by their suffering related to it.

Ishiguro's first novel, *A Pale View of Hills* (1982), is partially set in the devastated world of post–World War II Nagasaki, where everything and everyone is marked by the recent past. In his second and third novels, *An Artist of the Floating World* (1986) and *The Remains of the Day*, time is defined as "before" and "after" the war, and the main characters, narrators of their own stories, are defined in the same way as well. The first-person narrators of these two novels, Japanese painter Masuji Ono and the English butler Stevens, are reminiscing after the war about their prewar past and actions. Both ponder their own unwitting participation in the rise of fascism and in the "unleashing" of the forces that led to the war.

Ishiguro writes about life in peaceful times, but these are defined as before and after the war—as leading to the war and causing it or being profoundly changed by it. In Ishiguro's novels, periods of peace are not separated from those of violence. On the contrary, it is precisely this seemingly innocent peace that brings about and results in violence. The novel *The Remains of the Day* marginally mentions both societal forces and some politicians that participated in triggering World War II. Showing that politics is not entirely in the hands of a powerful few, however, the novel looks at "ordinary" people living their lives the best they can and explores how these lives contribute to the outbreak of violence. *The Remains of the Day* traces the particular mechanisms that made butler Stevens's perfect professionalism aid Hitler's policy in *inter bellum* Britain.

Butler Stevens helped bring about the concentration camps in his own "small way." In this chapter, the "dignified" butler Stevens and the Auschwitz *Vorarbeiter* Tadek, narrator of Borowski's stories, look at each other and see how they mutually define each other. Tadek would not be what he is without people like Stevens, who helped make his predicament possible, and Stevens would not be what he is without millions of Tadeks victimized in the war. Stevens and Tadek, Ishiguro and Borowski, do not tell two different stories: they tell one story of mutual interdependence and connection, a story of minute and indirect participation by individuals in the rise of fascism, of the present terrible face of the war, and of a posteriori reflections and suppression of a collaborationist's past. This chapter will trace connections between Borowski's *This Way for the Gas, Ladies and Gentlemen* and Ishiguro's *The Remains of the Day*, point out the few closures of power that these works articulate by reacting to them, and consider our own implicated position.

"A Day at Harmenz": "Objectification" of Oneself and Realistic Systematic Practices

"It is impossible to write about Auschwitz impersonally," Borowski wrote in a review of one of the hagiographic books about the camp. "The first duty of Auschwitzers is to make clear just what a camp is. . . . But let them not forget what the reader will unfailingly ask: But how did it happen that *you* survived?"[7]

Indeed, how did it happen that one survived? "The four million gassed, led straight from the ramp to the crematoriums, had no choice to make, nor did the prisoners selected for the ovens."[8] But Borowski's stories, drawn on the background of those millions of "the people who walked on," from the train to the gas chambers, are about the minority of those who were not led straight to execution.[9] A few of these prisoners managed to survive, and it is to them—and to himself as well—that Borowski poses a question: "But how did it happen that *you* survived?"

Borowski's story "A Day at Harmenz" gives one of the answers to this question, an answer whose relevance reaches beyond that of a specific historical event. The plot of this story revolves around a power struggle between Tadek, one of the *Vorarbeiter* in the camp and the first-person narrator of this story, and the Ukrainian Ivan, another camp *Vorarbeiter*. After finding out that Ivan was a thief who was stealing his things, Tadek orchestrates a complex mechanism of revenge that involves many people and various camp occurrences and that, as its final product, delivers a severe punishment to Ivan.

The story is narrated in the present tense, unfolding as it is being told ("I sit . . . we leave . . . I change . . . I give . . . I rush . . . I thank . . ."). The first-person narrator, Tadek, is also the main actor in the story. What is curious about Tadek's telling of this story is that he almost never mentions his subjective experience of what he sees or does. There are no exclamations of horror or loathing toward the camp's realities, which the narrator observes or participates in (as a *Vorarbeiter*) himself, realities of mass execution and slavery, torture, and starvation; he makes no expressions of fear or speculations on how it is possible that this "inexplicable" (*This Way*, 118) reality is happening, and no thoughts as to what he, the narrator—who is an active actor himself—should be doing next in situations that leave him some choice with regard to future action.

> The German got up from under the brick wall and took the watch from my hand.
> "Give it to me. I like it."
> "I can't, it's my own, from home."

"You can't? Ah, that's too bad." He swung his arm and hurled the watch against the brick wall. Then he seated himself calmly back in the shade and tucked his legs under him. "Hot today, isn't it?"

Without a word I picked up my broken watch and began to whistle. First a foxtrot, then an old tango, then the "Song of Warsaw" and all the Polish cavalry tunes, and finally the entire repertory of the political left. (59)

The above passage illustrates the way in which Tadek's "I" narrates the succession of events, including his own actions, as if he is observing them from the outside, from an external point of view that prevents him from seeing his own subjective response, his reflections, thoughts, or feelings. When a neighboring villager, Mrs. Haneczka, shows the "familiar looking" soaps she got from Ivan, for instance, Tadek does not actually state that he realizes these are the soaps that were stolen from him. Instead, he sketches the scene through rendering a conversation he has with Mrs. Haneczka, leaving the reader to make conclusions about discoveries that Tadek might be making at that point. In the same way, Tadek narrates his encounter with Ivan, during which he announces his intention to get revenge, by merely retelling what he saw and what he and Ivan said, and not by revealing his thoughts at that moment (aside from the brief mention that he felt nauseous).[10] And when he sees Ivan beating the elderly prisoner Becker, Tadek again just describes a scene in detail, not saying anything about his own perception of it. ("There, on the ground, lay Becker, moaning and spitting blood. Ivan stood over him, blindly kicking his face, his back, his belly" [72].)

Tadek's narrative thus constructs a peculiar division between a site of speaking and a site of seeing. While Tadek is the narrator of his own story, he views this story and himself from a site that seems to be outside of himself, a site that allows him to objectify himself and transform his "I" into one "he" among the others. This external point of perception allows Tadek to see himself within a wider system of power and as an element of this system, which is itself composed of mutually interacting elements. As such a "systematic" subject, Tadek maintains himself only through objectively mapping and remapping this changing system of power and his relations with other subjects of this system and through mathematically calculating, so to speak, his own best actions from the givens of this system. Borowski's poetic choice to leave explicit subjectivity out of this story is therefore due less to the documentary quality of this story or Borowski's sharing in the realist tradition and more to this story's articulation of specific "systematic" practices that allow Tadek to survive in the camp.

The seven parts of the story articulate Tadek's successive mapping of the changing field of power and his related derivation of his own actions. The story opens with Tadek's discerning the adversarial relation between himself and Ivan. The narrative then proceeds to describe a day at Harmenz through the things that

Tadek sees, does, or says and the power relations that he incessantly maps. He notes the relation between the big Kapo and the camp traders (they don't give him food) and also between Kapo and communism (Kapo is a sympathizer). By chance, Kapo thinks that Tadek is a Communist sympathizer as well and protects him from a German guard. Tadek reinforces this support relation by sending food to Kapo; he also sees Ivan in the possession of a stolen goose and finds out that Kapo was whipped because he could not find out who stole the goose. Tadek can thus conclude, without having to explicitly state it, that the relation between Kapo and the mysterious thief is that of Kapo's having a great incentive to find out who this thief is. While Tadek does not tell Kapo's boy that Ivan is the man they are after, he admonishes him to "keep his eyes open" and "see that some of the men catch geese" (67), thus alerting him to the fact that Tadek himself had seen these men.

In the fifth part of the story, Tadek maps out the relation of power outside of the camp: he hears the news about the Soviet occupation of Kiev. The sixth part is a divertimento from the main theme of revenge. Tadek shouts good news about Kiev to a few of his friends; a German guard hears him and asks for his serial number in order to report him. (Tadek has previously mentioned that he refused to give his shoes to this guard, which would create adversarial relations between the two of them; Ivan has a good relation with the same guard.) Tadek responds by instantly sketching the situation he is in and making a few correct responses. He quickly utilizes a nearby scene in which two prisoners are learning how to march with sticks tied to their legs, in his reply to the guard:

> "Excuse me, sir, but I think you misunderstood. Your Polish is not too good. I was speaking of the sticks* Andrei tied to the feet of the Greeks, over there on the road. I was saying how funny they looked." (73)
>
> *An untranslatable play on words. The Polish word for stick is pronounced almost the same as Kiev. (74)

Second, Tadek employs another previously noted relation, that between the guard and his fellow inmate Rubin. The two of them have traded before, so Tadek gives his watch to Rubin to give to the guard. These defensive strategies have worked and Tadek is called to thank "Mr. Guard" for not reporting him.

The seventh and final part of the story returns to the theme of revenge. Kapo's boy suggested the search of the prisoners; Ivan's Greek confidant is found in the possession of the goose and is not telling who gave it to him. The SS man says he'll shoot him if he does not talk. Ivan steps out, admits he gave a goose to the Greek, and receives severe punishment.

Both Tadek's offensive and defensive actions are "realistic"—that is, successful —when they are fully systematic, made by utilization of the various already existing relations among the system's elements or by the creation of new relations. It is crucial for Tadek to notice the relation between Kapo and camp traders, and to construct his own relation with Kapo on the basis of it. It is crucial to find out the relation between Kapo and *Unterscharführer*, who whipped Kapo on account of the stolen goose, in order to know that Kapo could be instrumental in finding a hidden thief. It is crucial to know of the relation between the inmate Rubin and the "dangerous" guard so that one can employ this relation in the appeasement of that guard. And it is crucial to always be maximally aware of one's environment and be able to use elements of that environment in the construction of one's defensive or offensive action, the way Tadek uses the scene of prisoners learning how to march in his defense against the enraged guard.

Realpolitik

The story "A Day at Harmenz" articulates the situation in which it is of existential importance to see and constitute oneself (in terms of one's practice) as an element of a wider system of power relations and not as a relatively separate and self-defined entity. We can call such practice *Realpolitik*. On the "macro" level of international politics, one can describe *Realpolitik* with the following:

> In its most extreme form, realism treats nation-states like billiard balls, whose internal contents, hidden by opaque shells, are irrelevant in predict- ing their behavior. The science of international politics does not require knowledge of those insides. One needs only to understand the mechanical laws of physics governing their interaction: how bouncing a ball off one cushion will leave it ricocheting at a complementary angle, or how the energy of one ball becomes differentially imparted to the two balls it strikes simultaneously.[11]

By constructing Tadek's practice as a rationally calculated element within a wider power system, Borowski's story "A Day at Harmenz" articulates the individual, "micro" level of *Realpolitik*. Tadek sees and constitutes himself as a "billiard ball," that is, from the "outside," mapping the structure of power and his own position within it. Tadek's practice is almost fully determined by his interaction with other subjects, and he sees his actions as if he were playing a systematic game of billiards, looking at how his striking of one "ball" (e.g., Kapo or Kapo's boy) produces the striking of another "ball" (Ivan), at which Tadek is actually aiming. All of the subjects in Borowski's story are constituted by this interaction, and their "internal contents" or their subjectivity—as long as they are not externalized by a material action—are very rarely present in the story.[12]

Tadek's few "unrealistic" practices are those in which he makes the mistake of insufficient self-objectification into solely an element of the power system and acts according to his own paradigmatic impulse. Errors occur when Tadek fails to constitute his practices "systematically." In part 2, Tadek provokes the *Kommandoführer* and has to be saved by the Kapo. In part 3, Tadek announces his intention to revenge himself on Ivan, and a warned Ivan counteracts by establishing a relation with Tadek's guard (in part 4), which shows itself to be a threatening one for Tadek later on. In part 6, Tadek carelessly vents his joy by loudly announcing to other inmates news about the Russians' taking Kiev and almost gets reported for subversive political activity.

When the mistake of turning to oneself happens, it is a rupture to which the subject does not give the time to form a separate presence (sentence) of its own. The mistake is thus often corrected within a moment of the same single sentence: "I feel an emptiness in the pit of my stomach, but I recover quickly" (73). Or "Without making the slightest move (he is a wild beast, I suddenly thought), without shifting my eyes from his face, I burst out in one breath" (75).

Borowski's story "A Day at Harmenz" shows that Tadek's nonrealistic subjectivity is not merely suppressed but not present during the performance of Tadek's realistic systematic practices. Also, although some of the power relations can and have to be mapped beforehand, Tadek's specific "calculations," which base his particular realistic practices, cannot and are not made before and outside of these practices themselves. An accurate realistic mapping cannot exist as a separate body of completed knowledge that is to be applied in a particular case. This realistic mapping can be made only in the moment of and with regard to a particular situation, structuring a unique set of elements relevant for this situation in a unique way.

In other words, Tadek's thoughts are not present in the story because they simply "do not exist"—as spelled out or well-articulated reflections—at the time of his actions. Realistic "calculations" cannot form themselves as any knowledge separate from practice, but only as these material practices—momentary material epiphanies—themselves. Tadek's construction of these calculated practices resembles that of a well-trained sportsman who cannot afford to think about his next move but simply does it, and the efficiency of the move shows whether it has been well calculated or not.

Any possibility of Tadek's basing his actions on criteria that are independent from the structure of power—whether these criteria be ethical or psychological—is abolished by Tadek's survival need to constitute his actions as systematic ones. "A Day at Harmenz" thus articulates the situation in which a person can survive only by fully becoming an element of the systematic power structure, a functioning part of this destructive power. As Machiavelli would put it, "the best come to resemble the worst" in order to survive.[13] Or, in Borowski's words, "We are not evoking evil irresponsibly or in vain, for we have now become a part of it" (113).

The Language of Realpolitik

In order to construct his practices as systematic realistic ones, Tadek must also articulate his environment in the appropriate language, which is as literal, undisturbed, and "objective" as possible.

> Becker's fingers tightened around the spade handle; his eyes began to appraise my body, my neck, my head.
>
> "You better let go of that spade, and stop looking at me with such murderous eyes. Tell me, is it true that your own son has given orders to have you killed." (54)

Tadek's economic language quickly appraises Becker's aggressive impulse and allows Tadek to promptly respond to it. The language of "A Day at Harmenz" is not primarily the result of an a posteriori decision made by the writer Borowski as to how to represent his past camp experiences. Rather, this language is inmate Tadek's means for the accurate and economical mapping of the power system and his position within it, a mapping that provides the basis for his material practices.

As a device for Tadek's accurate mapping of his environment, his language also reacts to and opposes the camp's own lies present in a destruction of semantics (e.g., "bath house" actually means "gas chamber") and theatrical cover-ups of the camp's real work. As one can see from the passages below, people to be gassed are pacified by being addressed as "ladies and gentlemen" and by the "kindly smiles" of SS men; tangos and fox-trots are played upon their arrival, gas chambers display the sign of a bath house, and vans transporting gas parade as Red Cross vehicles. The camp's destruction of literal meanings, that is, of the relation between signifiers and their signifieds, this deception of victims "until death," is a functional element of the camp's overall mission of human destruction:

> At the gate, a band was playing foxtrots and tangos. The camp gazed at the passing procession. . . . Slowly, behind the crowd of people, walk the SS men, urging them with kindly smiles to move along. They explain that it is not much farther and they pat on the back a little old man who runs over to a ditch, rapidly pulls down his trousers, and wobbling in a funny way squats down. An SS man calls to him and points to the people disappearing

round the bend. The little old man nods quickly, pulls up his trousers and, wobbling in a funny way, runs at a trot to catch up.

You snicker, amused at the sight of a man in such a big hurry to get to the gas chamber. (94–95)

"*Meine Herrschaften,* this way, ladies and gentlemen, try not to throw your things around, please. Show some goodwill," he says courteously, his restless hands playing with the slender whip.

"Of course, of course," they answer as they pass, and now they walk alongside the train somewhat more cheerfully. (38)

Somebody once called our camp *Betrugslager*—a fraud and mockery. A little strip of lawn at the edge of the barracks, a yard resembling a village square, a sign reading "bath" are enough to fool millions of people, to deceive them until death. (115)

As a man who has the chance to fight for his survival by performing accurate systematic practices, Tadek can construct his practices only with the help of a different language from that used by the camp, a language as "literal" and referential as possible. Thus, in order to construct his own reality, Tadek needs to be able to clearly state what is happening (who, what, where) at every moment. He also needs to omit all the possible subjective or emotional coloring of his language, leaving it as "transparent" as possible. In the following paragraph, Tadek's economic language rapidly maps both an easily discernible power relation and the awareness of how to act.

The *Rottenführer* approached and looked at us in the way one looks at a pair of horses drawing a cart, or cattle grazing in the field. Janek threw him a broad, friendly, man-to-man smile:

"We're cleaning out the ditch, sir, it certainly is full of mud."

The *Rottenführer* started and eyed the speaking prisoner with utter astonishment.

"Come here!" he said.

Janek put down his spade, jumped over the ditch, and walked up to him. The *Rottenführer* raised his hand and slammed him across the face with all his strength. Janek staggered, clutched at the raspberry bushes, and slid down into the slime. . . .

"I don't give a damn what you might be doing in the ditch. You can do nothing for all I care. But when you're addressing an SS man, take off your cap and stand to attention," said the *Rottenführer* and walked off. I helped Janek scramble out of the mud.

"What did I get that for, what, in the name of heaven?" he asked in amazement, utterly confused. (66–67)

As Tadek clearly sees it, Janek "understands nothing of the ways of the camp and probably never will" (66). This is not so primarily because Janek does not know how to address an SS man properly, but mostly because he fails to notice that the "*Rottenführer* looked at [him] in the way one looks at a pair of horses drawing a cart, or cattle grazing in the field." It is Tadek who quickly verbalizes for himself the *Rottenführer's* attitude toward inmates in a clear and direct statement, mapping the *Rottenführer's* relation to himself and Janek and deriving the knowledge of how (not) to act.

This referential and straightforward language precludes the intrusion of a more subjective discourse and thus allows the view of oneself as if from the "outside," the functional seeing and practicing of "I" as being one "he" among the others. Tadek only allows himself a minimum of "surplus" language in his conversations (e.g., irony present in the paragraph quoted below) but never in his formulations of the things that happen around him.

"A friend of mine was arrested for singing out of tune. You know, *falsch gesungen*. . . . Once, during a church service in Warsaw, when everyone was singing hymn, my friend started singing the national anthem. But since he sang out of tune, they locked him up. And they said they wouldn't let him out until he learned to sing properly. They even beat him regularly, but it was no use. I'm sure he won't get out before the war is over, because he's quite unmusical. Once he even confused a German march with Chopin's 'Funeral March'!" (65)

Different Literary Genres as Different Ways of Material Practice

Different literary genres articulate different ways of perceiving, knowing, and acting in the world, different aspects of reality or different realities.[14] Tadeusz Borowski directly or indirectly employs various literary genres in his concentration camp stories to articulate the divergent *modi* of an individual's practice in a place of ultimate material destruction. In Borowski's stories about Auschwitz, different genres articulate different ways of relating to or practicing the camp. Thus, "A Day at Harmenz" articulates a way of being in the camp different from that in the story "Auschwitz, Our Home (A Letter)," because the former story indirectly employs the mode of drama while the latter directly utilizes the genres of epistolary writing, travelogue, and essay.

The indirect employment of the genre of drama in "A Day at Harmenz" can be found in the numerous poetic characteristics of this story. Dialogues take up most of the story, while narration relates only the setting of the dialogue and the actions of the characters. The plot of the story is not constituted by a continuous narration but rather by a succession of dramatic situations; the seven parts of the story function as the seven acts of a play. Characters are constituted mostly by their actions and their speech. The story relates almost exclusively the visible practice of all characters (including the narrator), their speaking or acting, and almost never their thoughts or other subjective matters.

The dramatic mode of this story demands an "externalization" of Tadek's intentions. Thus, Tadek's decision to revenge himself on Ivan (at the beginning of the story) is not formulated as a thought he had but rather as a spoken announcement directed to an "empty space" (of a potential play audience): "'Just wait till I catch the thief,' I repeated, not realizing that I was talking to empty space" (52). Tadek externalizes this same intention once again in his dialogue with Ivan, thus making one of his few unrealistic (nonsystematic) actions: "You deserve more. Especially from me. And you'll get it, I promise you" (64).

"A Day at Harmenz" is organized around a conventional dramatic structure starting with conflict and ending with a resolution of this conflict, and displays the three classicist unities of a play: the unity of plot, time, and place. Most important, dramatic mode lies in this story's relational construction of the subject (Tadek) through his systematic practices. The Tadek of "A Day at Harmenz" is an actor in a drama of survival, completely defined by his relations and interactions with other characters, interactions unfolding in the present moment. The playlike form of "A Day at Harmenz" is also present in Tadek's "external point" of vision or his self-surveillance. Tadek has to split himself into the "audience" (who can observe all that is happening on the "stage" including Tadek's own position), on one hand, and one of the actors on the "stage," on the other hand, in order to see himself properly as only one of the many interrelated elements and in order to construct accurately his systematic *Realpolitik* practices.

Different literary genres articulate different shapes of power and consequently different constitutions of the subject within these power realms. In "A Day at Harmenz," the few "lucky" victims of the concentration camp (those who are not immediately executed) get a chance to be actors in a drama of survival and mutual power clash. In "Auschwitz, Our Home (A Letter)," some victims are shown as being even "luckier," freed altogether from the struggle for survival. These inmates are permitted the luxury of becoming observers, writers of essays and reflective letters, relatively uninvolved in the survival "play" of other inmates. Tadek as the subject of a play (in "A Day at Harmenz") relates to the concentration camp and practices it very differently than Tadek as a writer of letters in "Auschwitz, Our Home (A Letter)."

The Subject of Knowledge and Epistolary Writing

While "A Day at Harmenz" indirectly uses the genre of drama, the story "Auschwitz, Our Home (A Letter)"[15] explicitly employs the genre of epistolary writing, as well as other genres such as essay, travelogue, and autobiography. These genres articulate the paradigmatic constitution of a subject who has the privilege of being not one actor among the others in a drama of survival but rather an observer and thinker about the workings of power. "Auschwitz, Our Home (A Letter)" is written in the form of letters that Tadek writes to his fiancée, who is imprisoned in the women's section of Birkenau and who is repeatedly addressed in the narrative: "You know, it feels very strange to be writing to you, you whose face I have not seen for so long" (102); "Do you know what I am thinking about as I write to you?" (109).

The plot of the story concerns Tadek, the narrator (letter writer), going from Birkenau to Auschwitz for medical training. Tadek comes to Auschwitz for "schooling" and is thus freed from the usual struggle for survival that takes place in Birkenau.

> What delightful days: no roll-call, no duties to perform. The entire camp stands at attention, but we, the lucky spectators from another planet, lean out of the window and gaze at the world. . . . (100) . . . I roam around the camp, sightseeing and making psychological notes for myself. . . . (105) . . . I go on and on about the camp, about its various aspects, trying to unravel their deeper significance. (120–21)

Tadek is an observer of and "thinker" on the workings of Auschwitz but not an actor within them. As the subject, he is thus not determined by the system of power and its unbalancing (the beginning of plot) or rebalancing (the end of plot). He is not an element of a shifting systematic structure of power. Rather, he is a privileged "important guest" (114) and "lucky spectator from another planet" (100), an observer who establishes himself outside of the structure of power, which he sees and describes. Not directly claimed by the daily workings of Auschwitz, Tadek is able to constitute himself as a paradigmatic subject rather than a systematic one.

Tadek's paradigmatic self-constitution lies in the possibility of his developing a "surplus" of his practice over and above its being an element of a momentary structure of power and its constant rearticulations. This surplus practice lies mostly in Tadek's attempts to get to know and understand the camp. Tadek thus becomes a subject of knowledge who constitutes himself largely outside of the survival drama.

The "dramatic" mode of "A Day at Harmenz" is replaced in "Auschwitz, Our Home (A Letter)" by the mode of knowing and writing. Tadek can allow himself the luxury of not "practicing" the camp, but rather knowing or wanting to know and understand the camp and war through a "body of knowledge" separate from his own particular material practices. Tadek as a thinker tries to grasp "the essence of this pattern of daily events, discarding . . . sense of loathing and contempt, and find for it all a philosophic formula" (112). "I go on and on about the camp, about its various aspects, trying to unravel their deeper significance . . ." (120). "I think . . . I think . . . I think . . . And I think . . ." (110).

Tadek's constitution of himself as a subject of knowledge is paralleled by the similar constitution of the Auschwitz inmates. At the time of Tadek's visit, these inmates "have lived through and survived" (102) the worst period of their stay in the camp. Now they are not so much the actors in a drama of survival as they are the storytellers and "knowers" of past horrors and of their own past practices of survival:

> But the people here . . . you see, they have lived through and survived all the incredible horrors of the concentration camp, the concentration camp of the early years, about which one hears so many fantastic stories. At one time they weighed sixty pounds or less, they were beaten, selected for the gas chamber—you can understand, then, why today they wear ridiculous tight jackets, walk with a characteristic sway, and have nothing but praise of Auschwitz. (103)

> In Auschwitz one man knows all there is to know about another: when he was a "Muslim," how much he stole and through whom, the number of people he has strangled, and the number of people he has ruined. And they grin knowingly if you happen to utter a word of praise about anyone else. (102)

Tadek constructs his knowledge through the assembly of discursive elements (such as different genres, *modi* of language, various stories), which are independent of his realistic survival practice. The elements of knowledge are not connected by being elements of a particular structure of power but by being concerned with the same theme of camps, power, and war.

In "A Day at Harmenz," Tadek's material practice shapes various elements according to itself. Language, for instance, is thus brought to the level of the literal and referential language most suited for Tadek's survival practice. In "Auschwitz, Our Home (A Letter)," on the contrary, Tadek's quest for knowledge allows different elements to remain different, without being homogenized. Thus, this story contains a proliferation of various genres[16] and different modes of expression. While the narrator's language in "A Day at Harmenz," functioning as the medium for the clear mapping of the momentary structure of power, is as literal, referential, and "nonsubjective" as possible, the language of "Auschwitz, Our Home (A Letter)" is marked by internal rhetorical differentiation which articulates different aspects of the things the narrator attempts to know as well as different ways of "knowing" these things.

Tadek's letter can thus at times adopt an ironic attitude, emphasizing, for instance, the grotesque nature of Tadek's medical training: "We shall be entrusted with a lofty mission: to nurse back to health our fellow inmates who may have the 'misfortune' to become ill, suffer from severe apathy, or feel depressed about life in general" (98). In announcing the future of the world, his letter switches into a prophetic tone: "And we shall be forgotten, drowned out by the voices of the poets, the jurists, the philosophers, the priests. They will produce their own beauty, virtue and truth. They will produce religion" (132). The letter has comparisons and metaphors almost completely absent from "A Day at Harmenz," and many parts of it are rhetorically emphasized and transformed into a chantlike text through the usage of the anaphoric effect (consecutive sentences have the same beginning word), e.g., "We work . . . We carry . . . We are laying . . ." (131); "I think . . . I think . . . And I think" (110); "you are . . . and you are . . . and you are . . ." (118); "despite . . . and despite . . . and despite . . ." (103), and so on.

Tadek's survival practice in "A Day at Harmenz" employs the useful elements of the power realm and discards everything else. Tadek's quest for knowledge in "Auschwitz, Our Home," on the contrary, does not dismiss elements that are useless in material practice. Rather, knowledge is built precisely on the abundance and surplus of inserted stories, times, and spaces.[17]

The mutual relations amongst the characters of "Auschwitz, Our Home" consist mostly of their telling stories to each other about what they had experienced or witnessed, and their reflecting together on the "nature" of the camps. Not so much connected by present material practices, these characters are brought together by shared experiences and the telling and thinking about these experiences. Thus, the group of actors who act and react to each other from "A Day at Harmenz" is here replaced by the group of storytellers and thinkers:

> It is late evening—way past roll-call. Several of us sit around the table, telling stories. Everybody here tells stories—on the way to work, returning to the camp, working in the fields and in the trucks, in the bunks at night, standing at roll-call. Stories from books and stories from life. . . . [S]omehow today we cannot get away from camp tales, maybe because Kurt is about to leave. (124)

The paradigmatic constitution of the characters of "Auschwitz, Our Home," their storytelling, articulates the momentary surplus of subject over being solely a systematic function of the structure of power. The only character defined "systematically" in this story is the one who does not talk but rather does things, the one who has to perform the sole action crucial for the realization of story as a group of letters—getting the letters to their designated reader. This character is defined as a pure function of Tadek's need: he is the "feet."

> In order to reach their destination, these few pieces of paper must have a pair of feet. It is the feet that I have been hunting for. I finally located a pair—in high, red, laced-up boots. The feet, besides, wear dark glasses, have broad shoulders, and march daily to the F.K.L. [*Frauen Konzentration Lager*, women's part of the camp]. (140)

Tadek does not construct his knowledge by a systematization and homogenization on one level (e.g., of theoretical thinking)[18] but rather by fragmentary juxtaposition of numerous elements of various levels. He must employ all the forms of knowledge he can summon up in order to mark the multifaceted truth of the overwhelming reality he wants to understand and grasp some of the general rationale of the functioning of the camps and the camp's individual realizations of irrationality, irony, the grotesque, and tragedy.[19]

The juxtaposition of heterogeneous elements, which constitutes Tadek's knowledge in "Auschwitz, Our Home," dissolves the narrative, which as such was present in the practice-articulating "A Day at Harmenz." While language in "Auschwitz, Our Home" is still the language of realist narration, the inclusion of nonnarrative genres, extensive reflexivity, and the hypertrophy of subjectivity completely dissolve the narrative. The alleged plot of this story, Tadek's medical training, simply disappears: Tadek's training is continually postponed, and when it happens, Tadek writes very little about it. By dissolving the irrelevant narrative of Tadek's material practice, Borowski's story "Auschwitz, Our Home" articulates the subject of knowledge as the one who can constitute him/herself only in a power context in which s/he does not have to constitute him/herself fully or primarily as a subject of material survival practices.

This story's creation of a subject of knowledge of the war and the camps is the literary reaction to the incomprehensibility of the destruction that took place in the concentration camps. "Auschwitz, Our Home" reacts to this closure by constructing a model of knowledge and of a subject of knowledge. Tadek compares himself to a scientist who looks with "certain indulgence" at laymen who understand "nothing of how [the camp] functions" and who "look upon it as something inexplicable, almost abnormal."

> We saw some civilians: two frightened women in fur coats and a man with tired, worried eyes. Led by an SS man, they were being taken to the city jail which is temporarily located in the S.K. block. The women gazed with horror at the prisoners in stripes and at the massive camp installations. . . . But they are really quite amusing, these civilians. They react to the camp as a

wild boar reacts to firearms. Understanding nothing of how it functions, they look upon it as something inexplicable, almost abnormal. . . . Today, having become totally familiar with the inexplicable and the abnormal . . . having, so to say, daily broken bread with the beast—I look at these civilians with a certain indulgence, the way a scientist regards a layman, or the initiated an outsider. (111)

The model of "theoretical" knowledge constructed in "Auschwitz, Our Home," knowledge as a multifaceted profusion, conglomerate, or intersection of heterogeneous elements, is sharply contrasted at the end of the story with a different model of knowledge. Tadek returns to Birkenau and meets Abbie, an old acquaintance:

"So, you're still alive, Abbie? And what's new with you?"
"Not much. Just gassed up a Czech transport."
"That I know. I mean personally?"
"Personally? What sort of 'personally' is there for me? The oven, the barracks, back to the oven. . . . Have I got anybody around here? Well, if you really want to know what 'personally'—we've figured out a new way to burn people. Want to hear about it?"
I indicated polite interest.
"Well then, you take four little kids with plenty of hair on their heads, then stick the heads together and light the hair. The rest burns by itself and in no time at all the whole business is *gemacht*." (142)

Abbie is solely a functioning element of a destructive power structure—no "personal" surplus is permitted. Or rather, the personal aspect lies exclusively in Abbie's improvement of his functioning within a given power structure: "Well, if you really want to know what 'personally'—we've figured out a new way to burn people." Abbie's knowledge thus only concerns his enhancement of his systematic functioning. Juxtaposed with this kind of knowledge, Tadek's model of knowledge as a multifaceted intersection of heterogeneous elements shows itself (again) to be possible only as the knowledge of the past (made a posteriori), or the knowledge made by an outsider. The knowledge of present practices is a different one, in which the subject knows only how to perform or "personally" improve his or her own systematic practices.

"The World of Stone" and the Announcement of the "Immortal Epic"

"A Day at Harmenz" articulates the practices of a man who survives in the environment of utmost material destruction by means of articulating this environment as a sphere of *Realpolitik* and by constituting himself as an element of this sphere, an actor in a power drama. "Auschwitz, Our Home" articulates the more privileged outsider's constitution of himself as a subject of knowledge who tries to understand the war and the death camps, "this sudden frenzy of murder, this mounting tide of unleashed atavism . . ." (119). "The World of Stone," the final story of Borowski's collection, beginning with the reenactment of this shift from an actor in the past to a thinker and writer in the present, proposes "epic" as the next mode of subject constitution within the field of power.

> And I can see as distinctly as if I were looking in a mirror, the ruins, already overgrown with fresh, green grass, the peasant women, with their flour-thickened sour cream and their rancid-smelling dresses, the trolley-bus rails, the rag-ball and the children, the workers with their muscular arms and tired eyes, the street, the square and the angry babble rising above it into the restless clouds blown on by a strong wind—I can see all this suddenly float into the air and then drop, all in a tangle, right at my feet—like the broken reflection of trees and sky in a mountain stream rushing under a bridge.
>
> Sometimes it seems to me that even my physical sensibilities have coagulated and stiffened within me like resin. In contrast to years gone by, when I observed the world with wide-open, astonished eyes, and walked along every street alert, like a young man on a parapet, I can now push through the liveliest crowd with total indifference and rub against hot female bodies without the slightest emotion, even though the girls might try to seduce me with the bareness of their knees and their oiled, intricately coifed hair. Through half-open eyes I see with satisfaction that once again a gust of the cosmic gale has blown the crowd into the air, all the way up to the treetops, sucked the human bodies into a huge whirlpool, twisted their lips open in terror, mingled the children's rosy cheeks with the hairy chests of the men, entwined the clenched fists with strips of women's dresses, thrown snow-white thighs on the top, like foam, with hats and fragments of heads tangled in hair-like seaweed peeping from below. And I see that this weird snarl, this gigantic stew concocted out of the human crowd, flows along the street, down the gutter, and seeps into space with a loud gurgle, like water into a sewer. (178–79)

In "The World of Stone," the first-person narrator, a writer walking through the streets of postwar Warsaw, is neither an alert actor nor open-eyed observer. "In contrast to years gone by, when I observed the world with wide-open, astonished eyes, and walked along every street alert, like a young man on a parapet, I can now push through the liveliest crowd with total indifference . . ." The indifference to the reality he moves through, the "irreverence bordering almost on contempt,"

(179) is due to the narrator's realization that when he puts the mirror of his mind's eye to the present visible world of seemingly peaceful life, he does not see this peacefulness but rather a familiar destruction: "And I can see as distinctly as if I were looking in a mirror, the ruins . . . women . . . children . . . I can see all this suddenly float into the air and then drop, all in a tangle, right at my feet."

Such a distinct seeing of this other reality of "lips open in terror" makes the peaceful world of a Warsaw afternoon look as a passing and deceptive façade, a cover-up of its own imminent ruin. Having the vision of a "gigantic stew concocted out of the human crowd," the narrator cannot believe in the appearance of serene stability and consequently cannot get himself to act with reverence in this simulacrum world. He sees people making up everyday ordinary life—peasant women, dirty children, sweaty workmen—as being blown "once again" into realms that clearly transpose those of the concentration camps. These people are sucked into grotesque whirlpools or gigantic stews made of human bodies and tangled "right at my feet." The narrator's vision of the seemingly stable and stationary crowd of people being blown "once again" into the air by a gust of the cosmic gale is the vision of a "normal" life that in itself carries the seeds of destruction.

What is "normal" slides toward its own annihilation; what one does in one's everyday life cannot, "of course . . . keep the world . . . from swelling and bursting like an over-ripe pomegranate, leaving behind but a handful of gray, dry ashes" (179). Everyday life itself—this seemingly relatively solid, stable, and peaceful life—is a place that is "swelling" at this very moment and progressing toward its final "bursting," its self-destruction, which will leave behind, like in a concentration camp, only a "handful of gray, dry ashes."

The "world of stone" is an "unchanging" world (180) because its violence is not a historical contingency that happens by chance but an immanent consequence of the normalcy itself. Seen in such a way, the features of everyday life begin to resemble the deceiving façades of the concentration camps. The "normal" world is marked by a discrepancy between its present phenomenal level ("passers-by on the street below and the newly installed windows," "drunken singing . . . the shuffle of feet, the rumble of trains" [180]) and its latent destructive tendencies. Images of recent concentration camp experiences are thus not the stroller's free associations but the latent truth of this only apparently peaceful present life.

Rather than closing the collection of stories about the concentration camps by marking the immanence of violence in a world whose normalcy only disguises its destructive potentials, "The World of Stone" opens up Borowski's book with the announcement of a text that is yet to be written:

> And since today the world has not yet blown away, I take out fresh paper, arrange it neatly on the desk . . . and with a tremendous intellectual effort I attempt to grasp the true significance of the events, things and people I have

seen. For I intend to write a great, immortal epic, worthy of this unchanging, difficult world chiseled out of stone. (180)

Tadek's project is to write an "immortal epic" worthy of this "world chiseled out of stone," an epic in which he would "grasp the true significance of the events, people and things" he has seen. But how can he do that? How can he grasp the world, which is immanently that of destruction and violence, the world in which the "inexplicable actually happens"? (118). How can he write an "epic" of this world? And can he, actually, write this epic?

We can broadly define the epic as giving "form to a totality of life" (whereby "totality" means that only the whole of the world carries the truth, and all the particular and changing elements of the world are mutually connected) and as having as "its theme . . . not a personal destiny but the destiny of a community."[20] If epic articulates totality and community, then one can see that Borowski's stories define both totality and community in two different ways. On one hand, the totality is a "practical" one, achieved by the mapping of a momentary system of power with its structural causality[21] and relating systematic, *Realpolitik* subject-practices in the story "A Day at Harmenz." On the other hand, the totality is a "theoretical" one, made as an open-ended cumulation of different literary genres, various language modes, numerous stories, spaces, and times in the story "Auschwitz, Our Home." Community is articulated in two related ways as well: the community of people acting and reacting to each other as elements of an overall system of power, mutually related by their systematic practices, and the community of storytellers, mutually related by their shared experiences and the communication of these experiences.

The epic of Borowski's "World of Stone" should have two sides as well. On one hand, it should include the articulation of the overall power system(s) and structural causalities through which the subjects of practice interact. On the other hand, it should include the endless accumulation of various genres, discourses, stories, and so on, through which members of the collective communicate to each other their knowledge of "The World of Stone," the unchanging world of violence and destruction.

If Tadek wanted to write an "immortal epic" of the world, he could not write only stories about the concentration camps and their victims because he would have to articulate the totality of the overall power system that brought camps about and therefore include elements of the "normal" world that made the camps possible. Tadek's stories articulate the microsystems of the camp's power, but his epic would have to articulate the macrosystem of the world in which camps were only one element, brought about by the structural causality of the whole.

In order to write his epic, Tadek would have to complement his stories about the victims and the final execution of violence with the articulation of other elements of "The World of Stone," those elements that function as the structural causes of violence. Tadek's epic would also have to include a second aspect of totality and community, the aspect of the accumulation of various genres, discourses, modes of language, and so on, through which a collective communicates within itself the knowledge of its world.

It is clear that Tadek himself cannot write this epic. Only a collective could produce the endless accumulation of genres and discourses, and only a collective could map all of the macrosystems of power that produced the concentration camps. Tadek ends "The World of Stone" with the announcement of epic—and then nothing after it—because this epic should be collectively created by the readers of Tadek's stories. They should produce their own stories as elements of the same macrostructure of power, or the same epic, which they share with concentration camp inmate Tadek. This epic could subvert deceiving appearances that hide this world's immanent destructive potentials.

Kazuo Ishiguro's *The Remains of the Day* as One Story of Tadek's Epic

At the end of "The World of Stone," Borowski invites every reader to create his or her part of the collective epic by viewing the elements of his or her practice as being also the elements of epic Tadek calls for. In other words, the readers of Borowski's stories are invited to recognize the everyday practices of their own "normal" worlds as potentially leading to or allowing for the creation of violence that can appear in these readers' present time and space, but also in some other time or another space.

The British writer Kazuo Ishiguro can be seen as one such reader of Borowski's stories. Ishiguro writes his novels as elements of a wider epic of the "world of stone," an epic that is never directly thematized, but always indirectly marked and supposed in these novels. While Borowski writes about the victims of fascism, Kazuo Ishiguro writes about the ordinary people who were more or less direct supporters of the rise of fascism in the pre–World War II period. His novels do not depict the realities of the war, but they nevertheless always presuppose the reader's familiarity with them. These novels deal primarily with elements of an apparently peaceful and stable everyday life that have lead to mass destruction. Thus, they articulate a few parts of the epic of "The World of Stone" which they presuppose and share with Borowski's stories.

The Remains of the Day is the story of Stevens, a perfect English butler who helped Hitler's policies in England between the world wars in his own "small way" simply by serving his employer Lord Darlington the best he could. During the 1920s and 1930s, Lord Darlington had gone from criticizing the Versailles Treaty of 1919 to a brief association with the British fascist organization of Sir Oswald

Mosley, then to a prewar collaboration with Nazi Germany. Darlington carried on his political work behind the scenes; he organized an unofficial but highly influential international conference in his mansion, Darlington Hall, and he also facilitated a series of secret meetings between the British foreign secretary and German ambassador, meetings that took place in his mansion as well. According to butler Stevens, Lord Darlington genuinely believed he was doing the right and moral thing all along, and Stevens himself found it unthinkable to doubt or even judge his employer.

The story of the novel is set in the 1950s, when butler Stevens, the first-person narrator, weaves reflections about the present with memories of his pre–World War II work in Darlington's service. Stevens's narrative portrays himself as a perfect professional who takes great pride in his work and who consequently performed his service to Lord Darlington as best as he could. While Darlington went about achieving his goals through conventional political methods of meetings and networking, using arguments, debates, and the verbal level of communication in general, Stevens's own "perfect work," though nonpolitical in itself, ended up providing nonverbal and subliminal support to Darlington. Stevens's own instrument of influence was Darlington Hall, an impressive mansion, which, in Ishiguro's novel, assumes the features of a living and complex organism whose goal is to seduce an unprepared visitor into complacency with its master, Lord Darlington. Stevens manipulates Darlington Hall in order to produce an environment that influences guests and makes them more amiable and open to Darlington's suggestions.

In expectation of the 1923 conference, for instance, Stevens "set about preparing for the days ahead as . . . a general might prepare for a battle" (77) and then employed the many charms of Darlington Hall—"that magnificent banqueting hall . . . subtle, quiet soft light pervading the room"—to create an environment in which guests "lost much of [their] reserve" (98). During the course of Darlington's attempts to smooth out the objections that British foreign secretary Lord Halifax had on account of meeting German ambassador Herr Ribbentrop in the late 1930s, Stevens uses Darlington Hall's silver to change Halifax's unfavorable disposition. While on a "tour of Darlington Hall—a strategy which had helped many a nervous visitor to relax," Lord Halifax exclaims that "the silver in this house is a delight," and is, in Darlington's words, so "jolly impressed with the silver" that it "put him into a quite different frame of mind altogether" (135).

As Stevens says, "I never held any high office, mind you. Any influence I exerted was in a strictly unofficial capacity" (187). In his "unofficial capacity" Stevens indeed exerted influence by aestheticizing Lord Darlington's profascist policies and complementing Darlington's political work—which paved the way for the horrors of the war to come—with the aesthetically pleasing, "delightful," and "relaxing" forms of Darlington Hall, which put the visitors "into a quite different frame of mind altogether" (135).[22] Darlington Hall's aesthetically pleasing forms thus managed to efficiently hide the millions of deaths that were about to be claimed by Hitler's regime.

Butler *Stevens and* Vorarbeiter *Tadek*

Ishiguro's narrative mirrors Borowski's in its construction of an individual in the field of power in two ways. Stevens is both an acting insider (like Tadek in "A Day at Harmenz") and a thinking outsider (like Tadek in "Auschwitz, Our Home"), an actor and thinker. The parallel construction of the plot of Ishiguro's novel constitutes Stevens as a double or split subject. Present-day Stevens in his time off from service, traveling through England in July of 1956, is a thinker who remembers and ponders the past actor Stevens, who worked for Lord Darlington and actively contributed, in his own "small way," to the rise of fascism. The Stevens of today is a thinker and writer who looks upon his object, the acting Stevens of yesterday.

Stevens's past behavior mirrors that of Tadek from "A Day at Harmenz." As the subject of practice in the field of power, Stevens also constitutes his actions systematically. In the past, Stevens's practices upheld his professional survival and were constructed in relation to the system of professionalism. Many discussions Stevens and other butlers had over the nature of the "perfect professional" collectively mapped the *Realpolitik* structure of professionalism and the related realistic systematic practices. The "many hours of enjoyable discussion" (29) clearly pointed out which practices were "realistic" ones (allowing one's professional survival and ascent) and which were simply a product of "misguided idealism" (199).

> Indeed, Mr. Harry Smith's words tonight remind me very much of the sort of misguided idealism which beset significant sections of our generation throughout the twenties and thirties. I refer to the strand of opinion in the profession which suggested that any butler with serious aspirations should make it his business to be forever reappraising his employer—scrutinizing the latter's motives, analysing the implications of his views. Only in this way, so the argument ran, could one be sure one's skills were being employed to a desirable end. Although one sympathizes to some extent with the idealism contained in such argument, there can be little doubt that it is the result, like Mr. Smith's sentiments tonight, of misguided thinking. One need only look at the butlers who attempted to put such an approach into practice, and one will see that their careers—and in some cases they were highly promising careers—came to nothing as a direct consequence. I personally knew at least two professionals, both of some ability, who went from one employer to the next, forever dissatisfied, never settling anywhere, until they drifted from view altogether. That this should happen is not in the least surprising. For it

is, in practice, simply not possible to adopt such a critical attitude towards
an employer and at the same time provide good service. (199–200)

Realistic practices are those that avoid critical assessment of the employment
(appropriation) of one's own work. They do not allow a judgment of this appropriation of one's work, because "it is, in practice, simply impossible to adopt such
a critical attitude" (200) and perform one's work properly at the same time.

Then he [Lord Darlington] said:
"I've been doing a great deal of thinking, Stevens. A great deal of
thinking. And I've reached my conclusion. We cannot have Jews on the
staff here at Darlington Hall."
"Sir?"
"It's for the good of this house, Stevens. In the interests of the guests
we have staying here. I've looked into this carefully, Stevens, and I'm letting
you know my conclusion."
"Very well, sir."
"Tell me, Stevens, we have a few on the staff at the moment, don't we?
Jews, I mean."
"I believe two of the present staff members would fall into that category,
sir."
"Ah." His lordship paused for a moment, staring out of his window. "Of
course, you'll have to let them go. . . ."
In any case, to return to my thread, you will appreciate I was not
unperturbed at the prospect of telling Miss Kenton I was about to dismiss two
of her maids. Indeed, the maids had been perfectly satisfactory employees
and—I may as well say this since the Jewish issue has become so sensitive
of late—my every instinct opposed the idea of their dismissal. Nevertheless,
my duty in this instance was quite clear, and as I saw it, there was nothing
to be gained at all in irresponsibly displaying such personal doubts. It was a
difficult task, but as such, one that demanded to be carried out with dignity.
And so it was that when I finally raised the matter towards the end of our
conversation that evening, I did so in as concise and businesslike a way as
possible. (147–48)

There is a contradiction (which will be discussed later) between Stevens's
past actions (such as the "concise and businesslike" firing of two Jewish maids)
and his self-portrayal, which he constructs a posteriori by his narrative, whereby
he claims that his work for Lord Darlington was not guided by necessities of
professional survival but by the genuinely upheld belief that the impeccable work

in Darlington's service was indeed helping humanity. Despite what he might claim he thought or felt during his "realistic" past practices, however, in his work, Stevens indeed never allowed any subjective, uncalculated, ethical, or emotional "surplus" over and aside from his systematic self-construction. He fully identified himself as an element of the system of professionalism and refused any nonprofessional behavior that could distance itself from his systematic professional practices.[23]

> Lesser butlers will abandon their professional being for the private one at the least provocation. . . . The great butlers are great by virtue of their ability to inhabit their professional role and inhabit it to the utmost. (42)

Both *The Remains of the Day* and *This Way for the Gas, Ladies and Gentlemen* construct the subject of practice as the one who survives, either existentially or professionally, by constructing him/herself as an element of a given power system. Thus, Ishiguro's novel does not only thematize a part of Tadek's "epic" or of a structural causality of violence that made Tadek possible, but also articulates a more mundane version of Borowski's model of an individual's behavior in the field of power. Reading *This Way for the Gas, Ladies and Gentlemen* through "the eyes" of *The Remains of the Day* and vice versa, one can see how Borowski's stories provide a rather general blueprint of the construction of an individual subject within a field of power. These stories are about a unique historical event, but they also articulate a radical version, or an "experimentally pure" one, of a widespread self-constitution of the subject of power.

The Pseudoconfession, the Implication of the Reader, and the Collective Writing of an Epic

Butler Stevens's first-person narrative is shaped as an address to an imagined reader and made in relation to Stevens's own staging of potential queries, replies, and speculations of this reader. An interlocutor is mentioned at numerous points of the narrative: "But let me make it immediately clear. . . . But let me explain further" (5); "You may be amazed . . . but then you will agree"(9); "you will no doubt appreciate how . . ."(14); "you may not be aware . . ." (31); "I hope you will agree . . ."(42); "you may retort . . . but all I can say . . ."(43); and so forth.

Constructing itself in relation to a presupposed reader, Stevens's narrative acquires some of the attributes of a confession: Stevens admits (to "you") to having made certain decisions and actions that at the moment of confession, a posteriori, seem clearly reprehensible. Stevens's mode of confession presupposes the subject's self-constitution neither as a theoretical nor a practical "systematic" one (within the field of systematic power relations) but rather as a rhetorical one. "I" is being constituted by "I's" goal-oriented talking to "you." Stevens's entire narrative—all its elaborate argumentations and all its hard-labored explanations for Stevens's actions—is constructed as a rhetorical one whose goal is to be understood and sympathized with.

> It was that evening, shortly before dinner, that I overheard the conversation between Mr. Lewis and M. Dupont. I had for some reason gone up to M. Dupont's room and was about to knock, but before doing so, as is my custom, I paused for a second to listen at the door. You may not yourself be in the habit of taking this small precaution to avoid knocking at some highly inappropriate moment, but I always have been and can vouch that it is common practice amongst many professionals. That is to say, there is no subterfuge implied in such an action, and I for one had no intention of overhearing to the extent I did that evening. However, as fortune would have it, when I put my ear to M. Dupont's door, I happened to hear Mr. Lewis's voice, and though I cannot recall precisely the actual words I first heard, it was the tone of his voice that raised my suspicions. I was listening to the same genial, slow voice with which the American gentleman had charmed many since his arrival and yet it now contained something unmistakably covert. It was this realization, along with the fact that he was in M. Dupont's room, presumably addressing this most crucial personage, that caused me to stop my hand from knocking, and continue to listen instead.
>
> The bedroom doors of Darlington Hall are of a certain thickness and I could by no means hear complete exchanges; consequently, it is hard for me now to recall precisely what I overheard, just as, indeed, it was for me later that same evening when I reported to his lordship on the matter. (94–95)

Stevens's narrative claims an identity between his ethical judgments and his professionally realistic practices. This narrative puts a sign of equation between Stevens's alleged belief that his practices were "good" ones, and the *Realpolitik* of these practices. Stevens claims that he did what he did—eavesdrop and report on American politician Mr. Lewis, for example—because he had genuinely believed that he was doing the right thing. However, the rhetorical nature of Stevens's narrative, its pragmatic construction as an address to a reader, and its reader-oriented style sever the persuasiveness of this postulation of identity between ethics and professional politics. As a result, an identity between Stevens's postulated ethical beliefs and his systematic or realistic practices is dissolved. Stevens's narrative, repeatedly asserting his great desire of "serving humanity," falls back again into being a theatrical fashioning of a stage persona for the "you" of the reader. Consequently, Stevens's systematic realistic practices are revealed as nothing more than practices of professional survival (critical or less loyal butlers do not do well professionally). In its turn, Stevens's rhetorical casting of himself as a genuine ideal-ist (who might have been misled in his actions but had always meant well) appears as an aestheticization of his own *Realpolitik* practices, complementing his work that covered up Lord Darlington's profascist politics and mirroring the deceptiveness of the façades of the concentration camp ("little green lawns, orchestras") from Borowski's stories.[24]

While the construction of the subject of practice (as an element of a systematic power structure) in Ishiguro's novel mirrors that of Borowski's stories, Borowski's subject of knowledge (Tadek as the theoretical explorer of the camp) is replaced in Ishiguro's novel with Stevens as a rhetorical and self-aestheticizing subject. Tadek tries to understand the camp and all its features (including himself as the camp's functioning element), and always answers a question about his own survival. Butler Stevens, on the other hand, tries to hide his awareness of the way his past actions participated in the rise of fascism, not only in front of his potential interlocutors, but also in front of himself. His elegant language seduces and smooths over his guilt. This polished, comforting language is very different from the direct and economical one of practice-oriented Tadek in "A Day at Harmenz," or from the multilayered one of knowledge-oriented Tadek in "Auschwitz, our Home."

"But You Will No Doubt Also Understand What I Mean": Butler Stevens, Vorarbeiter Tadek, and the Reader

Stevens's confessional self-constitution is paralleled by the constitution of the "you" of the reader as an invisible judge of Stevens's narrative. However, Stevens constitutes this "you" as being not only a distanced arbiter for whom Stevens creates his convincing arguments and displays his basic innocence, but also as being someone who "would understand" and "no doubt appreciate" Stevens's actions. This "you" of the reader is implied by the "I" of Stevens: "you" is marked as someone who might consider, understand, and potentially approve of Stevens's practices.

> Even so, if you consider the pressures contingent on me that night, you may not think I delude myself unduly if I go so far as to suggest that I did perhaps display, in the face of everything, at least in some modest degree a "dignity" worthy of . . . (110)

Such a construction of the "you" of the reader does two things. First, it attempts to seduce the reader into complicity ("you may not think I delude myself"), and as such is a part of the "aestheticizing" moment of Stevens's text. Second, this construction of "you" also does exactly the opposite; that is, it displays the reader's own self-aestheticization in his or her automatic refusal of being implicated in any way by Stevens's narrative.

The latter aspect of the construction of the "you" reacts to, and thus articulates, the closure of the reader's belief that s/he is "outside" of Stevens's narrative and not implied by it. In Stevens's story, "you" can follow my narrative, understand my motives, agree with my reasoning. This "you" can identify with both Stevens's realistic systematic practices and his need to cover these practices with the intricate convincing discourse of basic good will and innocence.

By reacting to the reader's own self-aestheticization and refusal to recognize him/herself in Stevens's narrative, Ishiguro's novel implies the reader's "you" as sharing the same world as Stevens. The reader is invited to reflect on the possibility that s/he might have done the same as Stevens or else might even now be doing something similar: surviving by the performance of systematic realistic practices within given structures of power and constructing his or her paradigmatic or ethical being as partially or fully severed and independent from his or her realistic self-construction. Also, this reader's "you" is implied as making the same self-justifying aestheticizing texts as Stevens does.

Stevens's theatrical self-fashioning becomes a model of anyone's possible self-construction within a given systematic field of power, through realistic practices and justifying texts. The implied readers of Stevens's narrative are constructed as analogous to Stevens: their realistic practices, appropriated in various ways, may produce distant and potentially destructive consequences, and their self-justifying texts may cover up both those realistic practices and their destructive consequences.

Borowski's stories—read in dialogue with Ishiguro's novel—thus construct a radical version of these readers' systematic survival practices. Conversely, read through the "eyes" of Borowski's stories, Stevens's narrative becomes anyone's aestheticizing "web," which covers and closes rather than discovers and discloses these practices, and thus functions like the camp's façades, which "cover up" the real workings of the camp.

Ishiguro's novel works "against" Stevens's text by, as it were, putting this text into quotations and marking it as a speech with a clear rhetorical intention, that of the subject's self-denying misrepresentation and of the seduction of readers into complicity. Thus, Ishiguro's novel, like Borowski's stories, realizes the possibility of art to react to, and—through that reaction—reveal and display, the fictional cover-up and justification of realistic power practices. In their reaction to the closures of power, these two literary works articulate both the closures of survival practices and the aestheticization that participates in these practices, and thus function as liberating works that do not hide but rather expose the subject's self-constituting "realistic" modes and his or her self-justifying texts.

3

Literature against the Closures of Gender: Marina or About Biography by Irena Vrkljan and My Emily Dickinson by Susan Howe

> Poetry leads past possession of self to transfiguration beyond gender. . . . Poetry is affirmation in negation, ammunition in the yellow eye of a gun that an allegorical pilgrim will shoot straight into the quiet of Night's frame.
>
> —Susan Howe, My Emily Dickinson

In this chapter, Irena Vrkljan's Marina or About Biography (Marina ili o biografiji, 1986) and Susan Howe's My Emily Dickinson (1985) converse about the possibility of creating a woman whom "poetry leads to transfiguration beyond gender," to new realms of being and identity. The two works share the ambition of articulating these new realms of being that are pertinent for everyone, and their project is therefore not "only" feminist but also genuinely humanist in the broad sense of the word. Marina or About Biography and My Emily Dickinson have many common formal features: both texts are written by a woman poet about another woman poet (Marina Tsvetaeva and Emily Dickinson) who is crucial for the shaping and transforming of the writer's own life and poetry; both works experiment with forms of autobiography (Vrkljan's autobiography is at the same time a biography of Marina Tsvetaeva) and scholarship; both works are fragmentary and have the same precision of detail in imagining a space and time different from their own; and both display an attention to language which is that of poetry rather than prose.[1]

Both texts articulate woman as being, in her beginning phase, a reaction to the specific cultural closures of gender, refusing the given discourses and material practices that construct a woman. Given the differences between the cultural contexts of the two works, this initial step is also very different. While Howe writes in the North American context marked by a developed (though internally differentiated and changing) gender consciousness and feminist tradition, Vrkljan reacts to the closure of the nearly complete absence of the discourse of gender in the Yugoslavia of her time by articulating this category in her works ("I am a woman, I write about myself as a woman," and so forth). However, in her articulation of "woman," Vrkljan also reacts to (and articulates through her reaction) another closure that was characteristic of her cultural context, that of the predominance of group identity and consequent lack of individualism. A "woman" in Vrkljan's work can be created only through the simultaneous articulation of this missing individualism as well. "Splendor is subversive to the Collective will" (*My Emily*, 54). In *Marina or About Biography*, Vrkljan searches for an individuality that is not only a woman's appropriation of the modes of individualism predominant in Western cultures but also a radical redefinition and re-creation of these modes.

While Vrkljan reacts to the closure of group-based identity and the lack of individualism, Howe reacts to an opposite cultural closure in contemporary America, that of the abundance of women's confessional autobiography.[2] Howe never writes about herself in *My Emily Dickinson*, attempting to construct her text as a "silent" feminine Ear for the voices and sounds of a single Emily Dickinson poem, "My Life had stood—a Loaded Gun—," rather than as a translation of this poem into Howe's own familiar autobiography.

Both Vrkljan and Howe envision woman as a relational identity, constituted through her relation with the "other": Irena Vrkljan defines herself through Marina Tsvetaeva, and Susan Howe constitutes her writing as the reading of "My Life had stood—a Loaded Gun—." This relational identity, or transformative "love" relation in the basis of individual identity, opposes both objectification of others (as in a subject-object relation) and the voicing of oneself, which presupposes the silencing of others ("Conversion is . . . a falling into Love's powerful attraction" [*My Emily*, 79]). As such, the relational "love" identity is one of the potential foundations of a genuine community.

What *is* the communal vision of poetry if you are curved, odd, indefinite, irregular, feminine. (*My Emily*, 117)

And we lived communally. (*Marina*, 99)

Created by these two works, the relational identity—which at first seems like an answer to the problems of rampant individualism—starts showing its own problems; the dialogue between the two works has to continue its quest for the new realms of being and identity. Starting their voyage of discovery with a reaction to particular cultural closures of gender in their respective social environments,

Marina or About Biography and *My Emily Dickinson* go on to search—by means of their specific poetic practices—a new woman's identity that transcends gender and explores the space of a potentially different way of being.

Irena Vrkljan's *Silk, Scissors* and the Autobiography of a Woman: Gender, Individualism, and Politics

When Vrkljan's collection of autobiographical short narratives *Silk, Scissors* appeared in 1984, the public and critics received it as one of the literary events of the year.[3] In this work, Vrkljan speaks and reflects on her life. She writes about her Belgrade childhood in pre–World War II Yugoslavia, about her family's move to Zagreb in 1941, about World War II as seen through the eyes of her well-to-do bourgeois family unaffected by the war, and about her subsequent life in socialist Yugoslavia. We read about Vrkljan's work as a screenplay writer for Zagreb TV, about her marriage to and divorce from another writer, and about her stay in West Berlin, where she has been living most of the time since 1967. Even though Vrkljan wrote her *Silk, Scissors* after a longer stay in West Berlin, the largest part of this autobiographical book deals with Vrkljan's past life in Zagreb.

Vrkljan's book distinguished itself with a feminist tone that was atypical for its literary and cultural milieu.[4] In *Silk, Scissors*, an "ordinary" woman writes about her life and about the lives of people she knew, conveying her experiences, questions, and reflections on these lives. "My mother sits in one room on the fourth floor in Zagreb, and cannot express her anxiety," writes Vrkljan in the epigraph to her text.[5] Her work articulates some of the experiences of women who "cannot express their anxiety." Vrkljan asks, "What was it like, this women's life of ours in Zagreb?" (122) and writes about the "insurmountability of everyday life," a "non-existence of movement," and the "visiting of graves and preparing one for myself also" (139).

> [O]n the wall behind the kitchen cupboard there is a note: I will drown in a swamp. Nada cuts women's heads from the newspapers and magazines, tall stairs, clouds, and makes dark collages. (47)
>
> Various cafes, dreams of happiness, wrong movies of my youth, that whole slow life started to bother me, became physically foreign to me. . . . (55)
>
> Those who can save themselves, should do so. (56)

In her work, Vrkljan asks simple, basic questions and makes elementary statements with regard to the women's lot:

Are women helpless differently [from men] because they are alone in a different way, because they only cook and have children, and so there is no time for thinking, no time for conversations, descriptions of situations, we do not catch up with changes while new citizens are already getting our diseases? (123)

The education of girls. Sometimes submission with pleasure . . . (19)

Individualism and the Absence of Politics

Silk, Scissors takes one's self-constitution as a woman from the realm of commonality or solidarity with other women, the general realm of gender, to the realm of the individuality of a specific woman. By its articulation of a particular woman's individuality, Vrkljan's work strongly reacted to—and thus articulated through this reaction—the cultural closure of the lack of discourses of individualism in Vrkljan's cultural environment.[6] Vrkljan's articulation of a specific individuality does not concern only the individuality of a woman but rather attempts to reformulate the categories of being that relate to both genders and create the speech of individuality as such.

Silk, Scissors articulated a woman's speech about herself as a specific individual who is not fully expressed by the given modes of politics, work, or motherhood. Irena Vrkljan states that her writing is one of the ways in which she detaches herself from the background of the "generic" woman.

I'm putting down notes for tomorrow: buying oil, bread, writing a letter to a lawyer in regard to Vinka's residence permit, reading, talking to B. Writing. In spite of the noise in my head. (142)

Vrkljan's works were published in the 1980s, a period of the biggest post–World War II crisis in Yugoslavia, which led to the massive violence there at the close of that decade.[7] Given the autobiographical emphasis of Vrkljan's works, one could expect that the author would reflect on this unprecedented situation. After all, even though Irena Vrkljan has lived part-time in West Berlin since the late 1960s, she still spent a lot of time in Zagreb and the former Yugoslavia and could hardly have failed to notice the crisis that was developing there. However, even in narratives such as "City" (126), where Vrkljan depicts one of her recent visits to Zagreb, she does not mention the current crisis in any explicit way.

One could speculate that Vrkljan's decision not to write about the Yugoslav crisis of the 1980s and to focus on the private aspects of her life—the significant absence of politics in her work—was not a product of the lack of awareness about this crisis but rather a conscious poetic choice related to her work's attempt to articulate the speech of a woman's individuality. If Vrkljan had written about an aspect of this crisis—for example, rising nationalism—in an explicit way, the sheer weight of that topic at the time could have easily shifted the balance of the work away from the individual, unique, and so-far-unverbalized realms of existence and toward public, loud, and endlessly discussed political concerns. The work's attempts at creating a woman's individuality would have been gravely jeopardized. Vrkljan's project, in short, was not to add her voice to the already existing political debate but rather to point her finger at another reality altogether, whose very existence could defuse the potentially explosive situation of the public attention being focused on only one problem and only one description of that problem.

Working against the gross foreclosure of human possibilities inherent in the absence of the discourses of individualism, Vrkljan's *Silk, Scissors* attempted the articulation of this text of individuality and therefore had to avoid any direct mention of the current crisis. However, while *Silk, Scissors* does not explicitly thematize the crisis, it nevertheless deals with it by articulating one of the crucial cultural and political closures that caused and also characterized the crisis itself— the absence of individualism. Vrkljan's writing avoids the creation of a "generic" woman by being the writing and articulation of an individual woman, the author herself, through the texts of autobiography.

Autobiographies and Dictionaries

Opposing the cultural context of a group-based self-constitution, discourses, and practices, Vrkljan's autobiographical *Silk, Scissors* articulates the importance and the speech of one individual woman, the author herself. Vrkljan's work thus attempts to enact the "reverse" of the cultural processes in the historical formation of the Yugoslav identity, processes that strengthened group-based self-constitution as opposed to (the beginnings of) the individualistic self-constitution. With regard to Vrkljan's *Marina* and the literary tradition(s) of the former Yugoslavia, one could suggest that one of the many ways in which group-based identity was historically enforced resided in, among other things, the replacement of the eighteenth-century genre of autobiography—as present in the work of Serbian writer and educator Dositej Obradović, discussed below—with nineteenth-century dictionaries of the "people's" language. These dictionaries defined both the language one was supposed to use, as well as the practices—named in this language—one was supposed to engage in.

While national self-determination and the corresponding production of dictionaries of national languages were common features of nineteenth-century Europe, the radically antiurban, antiliterate, and anti-individualistic character of a dictionary of the Serbian language, made within a specific economic and political context, might distinguish both the dictionary itself and its functioning in the wider cultural context from the corresponding European phenomena.

Dositej Obradović's *The Life and Adventures of Dimitrije Obradović, who as a Monk was Given the Name Dositej, Written and Published by Himself* (1783) is a playful, wise, and exploratory autobiography that articulates the beginning of individualism: the "I" is important and has its own agency and text. This autobiography conveys the Enlightenment's assertion of the ability of the individual to think critically on his or her own (Dositej leaves the church and becomes a traveling student, teacher, and writer), as well as the cosmopolitanism of the creation of an individual's identity (as an intertwining of various different cultures) on the basis of Dositej's travels throughout Europe and Asia Minor.

In the eighteenth century, central Serbia was ruled by the Ottoman Empire (a case of Europe colonized by Asia), and Serbia's northern province Vojvodina, Dositej's home, was part of the Hapsburg monarchy. In addition to recounting Dositej's own unusually interesting and beneficial life, *Life and Adventures* also provides much ethnographic material on the life of the backward and oppressed Serbian people of that time. A large part of Dositej's autobiography is also a travelogue. Coming from the European margin colonized by both Europe and Asia, Dositej recounts his extensive travels through European and Asian countries, cultures, and political realities. Conversant in a dozen languages, Dositej also comments on his encyclopedic range of readings. Among other things, he discusses how his various readings and experiences in Europe and Asia relate to the colonial position of eighteenth-century Serbia. With regard to possible Serbian anticolonial practices, *Life and Adventures* both explicitly and by its formal characteristics promotes two principles.

First, national anticolonial self-constitution, while asserting "our" language and culture as opposed to the ones enforced by colonialism, is also based on an intense dialogue and interaction with other cultures, an eclectic and free appropriation of whatever one finds suitable in these other places for one's own project. Dositej's anticolonial project and writing are thus not based only on the promotion of "our" things, but also on the dialogical relation and dissolution of fixed differences between "ours" and "theirs" because foreign things can also be our own when accepted and appropriated in various ways and on our own terms.[8]

The second principle of Dositej's anticolonial practice and writing is the development of critical individuality. We (the nation or the people) should not liberate ourselves from them (the Ottoman Empire and Hapsburg Monarchy) in order to then enslave "I," an individual, by this newly independent "we." An individual "I" is not identical with "we" but rather in an uneasy relation of being in and out of "we" and of constantly changing this "we." Thus, Dositej's major work is his autobiography, in which he articulates an individual's—his own—specific understanding of nationally liberating anticolonial practices, undertaken with or without the others, and the individual shaping of potentially dialogical and relational character of national culture.

Dositej's eighteenth-century autobiography and cosmopolitan individualism are in the next century replaced by the assertion of "us," "the people," in arguably the single most important text for the Serbian language, culture, and literature of that era, *The Serbian Dictionary Explained by German and Latin Words, Collected and Published into the World by Vuk Stefanović Karadžić* (1852).[9] Karadžić's *Dictionary* and his work on national language achieved the task of promoting the popularly spoken Serbian language instead of the official Russo-Slavic, used only by the educated elite. While emancipating the popular language, however, Karadžić's *Dictionary* also dealt a blow to the "people's" Serbian language it was promoting. Namely, the words in his *Dictionary* were mostly only the ones that were actively used in rural settings; the "surplus" words used by the urban or literate population were mainly not admitted to this language. If one wanted to converse in the appropriate ("our") language and be a good patriot, thus, one could hardly use the term taken from someone's book rather than from a mostly illiterate rural population. One spoke "our language" only if this language was found as actively used in oral literature.

The words included in Karadžić's *Dictionary* are often defined by popular proverbs. For instance, "to be afraid" (*bojati se*) is matched with the proverb "Not every 'bad guy' is afraid of God, but he is afraid of beatings." The word "castigation" (*kar*) is explained by "Castigation does not make the head hurt"; the term "stinging nettle" (*kopriva*) by the proverb "The lightning does not want to hit the stinging nettle." The meaning of a word is fixed by a definition coming from the radically nonindividualistic group discourse of people's proverbs. Thus, as only a specific part of the population is defined as the "people," only one part of their language, that of oral proverbs or epic poems (oral literature) and active everyday speech, is defined as the "people's" language.

The *Dictionary* also explains in detail many popular customs, rituals, and everyday practices, thus giving precise instructions on how one is to perform and understand them. Therefore, the authority not only for the usage of language but also for the choice and performance of various social and material practices named by this language comes from the "people." Both language and practice are thus defined by the same source of meaning and authority in the *Dictionary*. Karadžić's postulation of the "people" (defined in this specific way) as the sole originator of the proper language and practice led to his being generally regarded as the founder not only of the modern Serbian language but also of the modern Serbian nation.

The final authority of "people" also strengthened patriarchal notions and practices. One could therefore argue that Karadžić's work, while contributing to national self-determination by emancipating the "people's" language, had also the negative effect of extinguishing both any nascent discourse of individualism and the potentials for the development of gender consciousness. In other words, Karadžić's work would probably have been more unambiguously emancipating in societies with developed discourses and practices of individualism. In Serbia, this work had not only a positive emancipating effect but also a negative effect, suppressing individualism and gender consciousness.

By creating a substantial body of autobiographical work, Irena Vrkljan could be seen as "holding out her hand" over the span of two centuries to Dositej Obradović. Vrkljan's autobiographical work, namely, should not be read as only a reaction to the absence of individualism in the recent history of post–World War II socialist Yugoslavia. Her work also reacts to the absence of individualism in the not-so-recent past, an absence enacted by, among other things, the replacement of eighteenth-century attempts of individualism and the genre of autobiography with nineteenth-century nationalist discourses and "people's" dictionaries.[10] Vrkljan articulates "woman" together with articulating "individualism," as (always) an individual woman.[11]

Two crucial aspects of this creation of individual woman related to the above discussion are (1) the reclaiming of the individual formation of words, away from group-based "dictionary" definitions; and (2) the dialogical or relational character of individual identity.

Marina *and the Biographies of Words*

Silk, Scissors begins Vrkljan's autobiographical and feminist project by simply stating "I": "I, an individual woman, am important." This collection of brief narratives chronologically recounts Vrkljan's life. Vrkljan's second prose work, *Marina or About Biography*, goes in a different direction and takes autobiography away from chronology or any other temporal or spatial order, away from one's own literal writing about oneself, and away from the referential prose of simply stating "how it all really was."

Marina also creates woman always as a specific, individual woman. The text constitutes autobiography and individuality by again reacting to, and thus articulating, the closure of group-based self-constitution. One specific aspect of this closure that *Marina* reacts to is the group-based determination of language and the definition of words.

The word is life. It is the beginning.
    And in it upbringing, family, homeland.
    Which bell do we always respond to? In our house the word devil meant sin. Devil—bell—sin. It was not like that for Marina. She loved the devil which sat on the bed in her half-sister Valeria's room. She loved him against the world of her mother, her nanny, against the world of religion. (19)

> The sun is yellow, the sea is blue. I learned all that obediently and obediently repeated it. . . .
> I did not emerge from that pattern even at fifteen. People are good and bad. Daddy is tired. Trees are green. These sentences revolved in me lethargically like a millstone through the long afternoons of childhood. (16)

"Sun" and "sea," "devil" and "people"—the words defined by a group (one's family and homeland) are given to a woman for her own unindividuated self-constitution. The way of individualism and autobiography (of both woman and man) lies in one's own specific appropriation of these words in speech and in material practices. "There is a biography of words," states *Marina* (23). By constructing her own individual "biographies" of specific words, Vrkljan attempts to appropriate the words from their dictionary and/or homeland-given group-based definitions:

> We used once to sit on that island of Brač with the painter Stančić on the lower terrace of his house. His face was swollen, we were waiting for the results of tests, his blood count, from the clinic. The sun was shining above our heads, and the cones in the pine trees were opening with a loud crack. . . .
> Together with the scent of pines a sense of danger stole up. Is it true that since then the pine no longer exists for me? Is it permissible only as it was up to then? The loud crack of the cones together with that swollen face? Those are questions about the path-ways words take. Or more exactly, about the path-ways of the loss of all imprecise content. Everything that is remembered alters the world from the point when something occurred.
> Pines, a face, fear. . . . (21–22)
> I should like to accept that for me the letters p i n e spell death, but . . . (23)

One's own "biography" of a word gives one's own specific meaning to this word: "pine" means death. In *Marina*, autobiography is constructed through the writing of one's biographies of particular words.[12] How I use the words and what they mean to me is who I am. "War," "exile," "poem," "kitchen," "pine," mean different things to me than to you; to me, they mean playing a piano and living undeservedly well as a child in Zagreb during World War II, desiring the "warm kitchen life" as opposed to the bourgeois "living-room" life in my grown-up years, the place of a friend's death filled with pines.

However, what words mean to me—and who I am—is not exhausted solely by my own biographies of the words. These biographies mark my limitation and lack of freedom within the space of that which I myself lived through, the space of "terrible: this is how it was" (24). But the words might mean to me otherwise from what my own biographies of the words, biographies based on the words' materializations in my past, would allow them to. The words ("I," "woman") have the potential of "openness," of acquiring different meanings. Therefore, I, an individual woman—and my autobiography—could be otherwise as well. "Much of what I can do today depends on whether I do not have to remember" (28).

> I should like to forget all questions about facts. I should like to accept that for me the letters p i n e spell death, but that there are thousands of other pines. False definition through words—are these questions for a biography? (23)

One can be "wrongly determined" through one's own biographies of words. Thus, the space of freedom is the space where my words—and I—are not determined solely by myself and by that which is in my "present [and] proximity," the space where my definitions of words meet others' definitions (biographies, stories) of words: "Into the distance, into form, into stories told to others" (25). My words are constituted not only through my own biographies of them—the space of the past reality of "this was so" and of the limitations and definitiveness of this past— but also through others' definitions of them and through my conversation with these other articulations of "my" words.

Created through my conversation with others, the "space of freedom" of my words can be many things: it can be the space of potential of my different future being, but also the space of creation of a different perception of my own past. For example, Vrkljan grasps the word "melancholy," which depicts an aspect of her own childhood, through the creation of a conversation among Vrkljan's own memories, the attitude of Vrkljan's friends, and the paintings and words of Charlotte Salomon.

> So I am standing in the room, and mother is putting or not putting something into a cupboard, listening, or not listening. Inattentiveness, the melancholy of non-concentration. I stand and lethargy drifts through the room. No interest in anything at all. (26)
>
> Recently, a long conversation about the melancholy of bourgeois women. And about the fact that, whatever we offer or do, we cannot help at all. Hence also the coldness of melancholy. A life lived in images. This brings destruction, the loss of reason, death, and nothing is changed. A little art, a little love, a little life, says the painter Charlotte Salomon. And she draws little girls in rooms in various towns. She draws right up to 1939 when the Germans find her in occupied France and send her to a camp, where she dies. The pictures remain, more than 700 pictures of melancholy in her family. (25–26)

If "I" am my words and my words are always defined through conversation with others' "biographies" of words, then "I" myself am always this conversation and interaction with other people. "I" is always "the others" as well, and thus "my" autobiography becomes a biography of others:

> The biographies of others. Splinters in our body. As I pull them out, I pull out my own pictures from a deep, dark funnel. (33)

Individuality as Togetherness

In *Marina*, Vrkljan constructs her autobiography by writing the biography of Russian poetess Marina Tsvetaeva, as well as parts of biographies of many other men and women (including Irena Vrkljan herself), from both the "East" and the "West."

> I yearn for Marina. A Russian poet, born 1892, committed suicide in Elabuga, 1941. (13)
>
> Dora, Marina and I. Three women saying farewell. Or arriving somewhere, where the sun still shines. (14)

Vrkljan's *Silk, Scissors* articulates an initial act of opposition to the sociocultural context of a group-based and patriarchal self-constitution by the articulation of an "individual woman." *Marina*, Vrkljan's second autobiographical work, articulates the next step of the formation of individuality. In *Silk, Scissors* "I" say myself ("I am 'I,' unique and different") by pulling myself out of the collective "we are" ("'we' are all equal and same"). But individuality and "I" created in this way could become limited within the boundaries of solipsism and self-centeredness.

The fulfillment of "I" does not lie only in this assertion of myself. *Marina* explores a dialectic of individualism, whereupon, after asserting its own distinctiveness from the "we," "I" searches for the ways of again being connected with others and overcoming its own isolation. Therefore, while *Silk, Scissors* makes the initial move of separating "I" from the others, *Marina* reacts to the resultant closure of individualism itself through its articulation of "togetherness" as the bedrock of an individual.[13] "[N]either autobiography nor biography, but a mixture of both, with the two strands inextricably linked."[14]

Marina articulates individuality as togetherness by creating the text of an autobiography—the text of an individual—that is a collage comprised of numerous fragments from Vrkljan's own and other people's biographies. "I on You, fused, in a new, third, rhyme" (9). The juxtaposition of fragments explodes the unity of one distinctive character (Vrkljan) and her distinct biography, as well as the chronological ordering of time.

> The past lives in us without chronology. Everything is simultaneously here, all colours, all feelings. . . . Every book about life could run parallel, in columns, it could express the whole if we were not brought up to believe in sequences, in hierarchies. Important, unimportant. Beginning, end. . . . Physical death as the final point of a story, a life. The past, the future, rising, falling lines. I do not want to write for that death. I should like to repeat Marina's question: who will break the clock and so free us from time? (55)

The montage of *Marina* also defies spatial (here versus there) and logical rules ("'I' am not 'not-I'"). This work intertwines fragments of many lives, including those of Irena Vrkljan, Marina Tsvetaeva, Croatian painter Miljenko Stančić, surrealist Ljubiša Jocić, German writer Rainer Maria Rilke, Italian writer Elsa Morante, Russian writers Pasternak and Beli, as well as moments from different times. The assemblage of various fragments that are "factually" separated by time, space, and the (Aristotelian) logic of things does not create a linear narrative; rather, these fragments create a space of togetherness in which the parts of your and my lives and texts interrelate.[15]

> When Marina passes through the room (and she would if she still existed), she always has paper, a pencil and a note-book in the deep pocket of her apron. And I hear her words: "I have settled completely into my note-book."
> Dora sits in a house in Zagreb and says nothing any more. Her spirit left that room five years ago. And where did I move to? Was it only to another country? A divided life, a bit in Zagreb, a bit in Berlin, one part devours the other. . . .
> Kafka writes on 30 November to Felice: "They can't drive me altogether out of writing as I have already thought several times that I am sitting in its midst, in its best warmth."
> Felice Bauer lived in Wilmersdorf street in Berlin, a few steps from the building where I am writing this. Her house was destroyed in the war, now there is a department store selling men's clothes where it stood. Places for flight and passing through. Berlin. The crossroads of biographies. Marina and Kafka could have met. In 1922 she left Berlin for Prague, in 1923 he moved from Prague to Berlin. (34–35)

Past is put together with present, here with there; you who are far away in space and time are here and now in *Marina*, and I defy the logic of identity by also being this "you." In some moments, *Marina*'s "I" is the product of a contact and relation between "you" and "me"; in other moments, the "I" is almost schizophrenically identical with "you."

> The second-hand bookshop where my first husband worked was one such place. Full of darkness, books and dust . . . [I]n the safe . . . there was a first edition of the *Metamorphosis* as well, Leipzig 1915. . . .
>
> Marina read Kafka. Someone has described how, when she was living as an emigrée, she was once interrogated in a Paris police station about Sergei Efron's alleged spying activities, instead of replying she simply recited her poems and parts of Kafka's *Trial*. She said nothing else.
>
> *The simultaneity* of remembrance. The police station building in Paris, a book in the Zagreb shop, accusations, misunderstandings, the same dull light. (29–30)

As mentioned above, individuality as togetherness, the creation of "I" through my being with others, parallels the constitution of my words through my conversation with others ("what words mean to me is who I am"). The space of my contact with others is the space of my potential freedom from the limitations of (only) "I" and (only) my own "biographies" of my words. If my words and "I" are created through contact with others, my autobiography is also always the biography of others.

Writing as Reading

Vrkljan's writing is a reading of Tsvetaeva's life, and a rewriting of this life. A woman's individuality as togetherness and contact with others is created by the writing of oneself that is at the same time the reading of other people's lives and texts. Such a balance of reading and writing, of listening and talking, is connected with the "individuality as togetherness" that Vrkljan attempts to articulate. In *Marina,* a woman constitutes herself not as one "monad" separated from the others but rather as an identity composed of fragments of "other" people whom a woman "reads," imagines, and has a sympathetic relationship with.

> Marina. That name brings also the thought of a date. A date in 1941. In a distant country, in the unknown town of Elabuga. 31st August 1941. Why did a woman have to die that day? (33)
>
> August 1941: the last Jews of the town of Zagreb are sent away to camp. On 31st August at home we celebrate my mother's birthday. (105)

Marina and Mur [Marina's son] are sitting in a train. The journey in the summer of 1941 to Elabuga. Moscow is being evacuated, the train is full of refugees. (94)

My mother exchanges a ring for a loaf of bread. That was during the flight to Zagreb, in 1941. We are traveling in a crowded train, children are shouting, women weeping. What is repeated are pictures. But not the content. (95)

By constituting individuality as "togetherness" and by balancing the writing of oneself with the reading of others, *Marina* reacts to and thus articulates the closures of individuality not only as separateness of "I" from the "others" but also as subject-construction in which one creates oneself through silencing the others. *Marina* constitutes one woman's individuality not by silencing but rather by voicing the others. Self-constitution is the constitution of others; it fosters rather than suppresses the realization of others who create "me." The reading as writing of others creates others who create "me." Individuals are "each other's central source. They contain, define, and defy one another, and everyone else around them" (*My Emily*, 136).

The balance of reading and writing in *Marina* marks a space in which "I" can be a writer only by being a reader. Namely, "I" read the others' constitution of their words and of their lives, and my own autobiography and self-constitution in freedom is created through this contact with others' constitution of words and lives. The possibilities of my freedom (which includes, but is not limited to writing) are named in the space where "my" biographies of words ("life," "poet," "woman") meet others' biographies of these words.

The Cross-Cultural Identity

Individuality as "togetherness" also presupposes an identity created through on-going contact among various national cultures rather than through the adherence to only one's "own" culture. Vrkljan quotes Tsvetaeva: "World is our world . . . / Not tongue-less, but all-tongued" (6). Vrkljan herself is a point of crossing of various national cultures: she grew up bilingual (Croatian/Serbian and German), lived in the former Yugoslavia for the first thirty-six years of her life, and has been living part-time in West Berlin since 1967. A foreigner in Germany yet never seeming to have felt at home in Yugoslavia either, Vrkljan wrote and published *Silk, Scissors* first in German (under the title *Tochter zwischen Süd und West*) and then in the Croatian language, and she writes her autobiography through the writing/reading of a biography of a Russian poetess: "From then on an attempt to live in two countries. Writing in between" (49).

Vrkljan's choice of writing about a Russian poet rather than a Yugoslav one— her showing that this poet speaks to or about her just as much or more than any of her "national" poets—enacts an opposition to any sort of nationalist isolationism. Vrkljan marks the cross-cultural nature of her own autobiography at the very beginning of *Marina:* she starts the book with a translation of Tsvetaeva's poem "New Year Letter" dedicated to the German poet and Tsvetaeva's close friend Rainer Maria Rilke, and she thanks Ina Tinzman, a woman from Munich, for her help with reading and translating the Russian texts.

Individuality as togetherness causes the "foreign" to become most intimately mine, the space of freedom of potentially different realizations of "I." One of the examples where this liberating dynamic enacts itself is in Vrkljan's attitude toward music. The word "piano" marks a past of oppressive bourgeois upbringing for Vrkljan (the enforced piano lessons) and also indirectly suggests one of the possible reasons for the absence of the theme of music in Vrkljan's writings, otherwise filled with reflections of other arts.

> I had to play [piano] for two hours a day, Father sat beside me with a watch in his hand. That practice seemed endless, I made no progress at all. . . . My hands were small and the new teacher did not believe I would ever play well. (38)

Through the reading of Tsvetaeva's writings, however, "piano" becomes a symbol of something one mourns for the most when dying: "I regret only the sun and music," says Tsvetaeva's dying mother, a brilliant and passionate piano player (108). Through contact with Tsvetaeva's writings, both the word "piano" and music in general are released from one's own lack of freedom of the (auto)biographical and factual past and into a freedom of a potentially different being: piano and music can be different than they were for me; thus, piano (music) and I could, perhaps, still be different.

That which is different from me helps me move, change, and "come into being"; is a missing part of me. The relation toward the "other" in Vrkljan's prose is not a relation of a subject toward an object but rather a relation of an unfinished, lacking subject toward the missing part of self that is finally found and is now read through the infinite care of patient listening.

Echoing between *My Emily Dickinson* and *Marina*

Irena Vrkljan constitutes her autobiography through writing Marina Tsveaeva's biography. Susan Howe creates *My Emily Dickinson* as a reading of one of the most famous poems by nineteenth-century American poet Emily Dickinson, "My Life had stood—a Loaded Gun—."

> My Life had stood—a Loaded Gun—
> In Corners—till a Day
> The Owner passed—identified—
> And carried Me away—
>
> And now We roam in Sovreign Woods—
> And now We hunt the Doe—
> And every time I speak for Him—
> The Mountains straight reply—
>
> And do I smile, such cordial light
> Upon the Valley glow—
> It is as a Vesuvian face
> Had let it's pleasure through—
>
> And when at Night—Our good Day done—
> I guard My Master's Head—
> 'Tis better than the Eider-Duck's
> Deep Pillow—to have shared—
>
> To foe of His—I'm deadly foe—
> None stir the second time—
> On whom I lay a Yellow Eye—
> Or an emphatic Thumb—
>
> Though I than He—may longer live
> He longer must—that I—
> For I have but the power to kill,
> Without—the power to die—

While Vrkljan reacts to the absence of both gender consciousness and individualism by the creation of the individual woman through her autobiographical texts, Howe works in the American context of a developed gender consciousness and has to react to an almost opposite cultural closure of the abundance of women's auto/biographical writing. Thus, in opposition to Vrkljan's writing about Marina Tsvetaeva through writing about herself (and vice versa), Howe omits any autobiographical interjections in *My Emily Dickinson*.

Individualized Words: Connotations and Contact Zones

Regardless of the culturally based difference between Vrkljan and Howe in their creation of a woman, both writers articulate a woman as a relational identity.

Also, Howe constructs Dickinson's poem by using some of the same strategies employed by Vrkljan in her construction of her own/Marina Tsvetaeva's life. Vrkljan's constitution of the individualized and individualizing words ("how I use the words and what they mean to me is who I am"), words that transcend the realm of the collective's dictionary-based definitions, is matched by Howe's construction of Dickinson's individualized words and motives.

The poet's words are again conceptualized as fleeing the realm of dictionary and group definition: "Poet . . . deeper region of herself—a maples dominion, valueless value, sovereign and feminine, outside the realm of dictionary definition . . ." (*My Emily*, 111). Vrkljan's creation of the "biographies" of her own and Tsvetaeva's words, of these words' idiosyncratic constitution by an individual subject (herself and/or Tsvetaeva), a subject who herself is constituted through constitution of her words ("war," "mother," "pearl"), is paralleled by Howe's search for the idiosyncratic "biographies" of Dickinson's words and motives.

Howe's text constructs the "biographies" of Dickinson's words through a two-fold strategy. The first aspect of this strategy involves the sympathetic reconstitution of some of the connotations with which Dickinson might have entrusted her words given her historical context. For example, Howe begins the construction of the "biography" of Dickinson's word "Eider-Duck" (from the lines " 'Tis better than the Eider-Duck's / Deep Pillow—to have shared—") with a description of a significant characteristic of this bird: "The female eider plucks from her breast the down that lines her nest" (109). The "biography" of the word "Eider-Duck" then goes on to the narration of the destiny of that bird in Dickinson's time.

> In North America, the birds were killed for their feathers, as their flesh was considered worthless. By the late eighteenth century Eiders were so rare that even feather hunting was considered a waste of time and profit. Eider-down was imported from Europe.
> Still, hunters and fishermen killed the birds for sport, and for their eggs. By the end of the 1800s the vast Eider nurseries of the Labrador Coast were only a legend. In Dickinson's time, the Eider was rare but not extinct. Massachusetts gunners called them Sea Ducks. (109)

After outlining the progressive extinction of eider ducks in Dickinson's time, Howe goes on with her reading of Dickinson's poem and the poet herself.

> Deep Pillow was a warm bed and safe house if Dickinson took Higginson's advice and altered the eccentricity of her poems to suit the taste of her time. . . . A newly married wife shares her pillow with her husband even if what she rests her head on is the freedom she has plucked from her own breast. . . . Deep calls to Deep, suggesting death and drowning. (109)

Dickinson's individual "biography" of the word "Eider-Duck" then proceeds to become constructed by the second aspect of the strategy that Howe uses in the creation of the "biographies" of Dickinson's words. This aspect lies in the re-creation of the "contact zone" in which Dickinson's words got shaped through the poet's dialogues with her readings:

> Emily Brontë's persona Catherine Linton, driven mad by her inability to detach Heathcliff from herself, and remorse over marrying Edgar, echoed Ophelia. Dickinson's two lines echo Catherine.
>
> > Tossing about, she increased her feverish bewilderment to madness, and tore the pillow with her teeth . . . . she seemed to find childish diversion in pulling the feathers from the rents she had just made, and ranging them on the sheet according to their different species . . . . " . . . . and this . . . . it's a lapwig's. Bonny bird . . . . Heathcliff set a trap over it, and the old ones dare not come. I made him promise he'd never shoot a lapwig, after that, and he didn't. Yes, here and more! Did he shoot my lapwigs, Nelly? Are they red, any of them? Let me look." (109–10)
>
> Deep Pillow slides in another echo of an echo, Keats' "Bright Star." (111)

Howe's text constructs the "biography" of Dickinson's word "Eider-Duck" by making explicit some of the multiple threads woven into this word. The example of "Eider-Duck" shows a typical two-fold strategy of Howe's text. On one hand, the "biographies" of Dickinson's words are made through "archaeological"[16] excavation of the various aspects of Dickinson's historical and cultural context (such as the legacy of Calvinism and its brilliant philosopher Jonathan Edwards, the aspects of the world of the first settlers or Massachusetts in the time of Dickinson's life) and related connotations of Dickinson's words. On the other hand, the "biographies" of words are constructed through re-creation of the space of transformative contact between Dickinson and her readings (e.g., Browning, Shakespeare, Emily Brontë).

Howe's two-fold strategy of constructing the "biographies" of Dickinson's words mirrors Vrkljan's construction of the "biographies" of her own and Tsvetaeva's words. Howe's archaeological "excavation" of specific cultural and historical traits of Dickinson's context is refigured in Vrkljan's bringing of the personal, political, and cultural history that contributed to the creation of her and Tsvetaeva's "biographies" of words. Howe's creation of the space of contact between Dickinson and her readings, a contact that also shaped Dickinson's words, refigures Vrkljan's creation of the space of conversation among her and others' "biographies" of words, a conversation that, in its turn, shaped Vrkljan's own words. (For instance, Vrkljan's word "piano" changes through her reading of Tsvetaeva's writings on this word.)

The Spirit Is the Ear

Howe constructs "biographies" of Dickinson's words by turning her text into a "Spirit of the (feminine) Ear" for Dickinson's poem. Emily Dickinson writes:

> The Spirit is the Conscious Ear.
> We actually Hear
> When We inspect —that's audible—
> That is admitted—Here—
>
> (22)

Howe's "writing of the ear" has to hear everything that is audible "inside the space" of Dickinson's poem, and that which is audible is posed in Howe's text as that which Dickinson's poem relates to, as the other end of the poem's numerous relations. The "ear" of Howe's text is conceived as simply receiving those elements from the "other end" of the poem's many relations. Thus, the exhaustive literary and historical network surrounding Dickinson's poem is constructed as if Howe's text merely yielded to the presence of sounds and meanings that could not be avoided because they were "audible."

Howe's "Spirit of the Ear" records many relational sounds in the room of Dickinson's poem "My Life had stood—a Loaded Gun—," including the echoes of "Dante, Chaucer, Spencer, Shakespeare, Donne, Milton, Keats, Shelley, Wordsworth, Tennyson" (106), Jonathan Edwards, Emily Brontë, Dickinson's Massachusetts, and many other things. These sounds constitute the "biographies" of Dickinson's words, and these "biographies" become, in their turn, one of the constituent elements of the "Architecture of Meaning"[17] of Dickinson's poem and of Emily Dickinson herself: "The Eider-Duck has torn apart all interpretation of place and progress in Dickinson's poem" and "Emily Dickinson knew that sharing the Duck's Deep Pillow would have meant slaying her own genius" (110).

Women's Relational Identity

Like Vrkljan's *Marina*, Howe's text also parallels the construction of Dickinson's words and writings as relational ones (created through contact with others' words and writings) with the construction of a woman's identity as a relational one as well. Howe constitutes her text (and by implication a woman's identity) as the reading/writing of Dickinson's poem ("*my* Emily Dickinson"), and this poem itself is interpreted as articulating the "unity [of two beings] at the core of identity" (136). Thus, the woman's "identity" articulated by both Howe's text and Dickinson's poem is a relational one.

"Connections between unconnected things are the unreal reality of Poetry," writes Howe (97), and also "Myself was as another, now 'I' dare to go farther" (61). The relation between Howe's text and Dickinson's poem is refigured in relation between Dickinson's poem and Emily Brontë's *Wuthering Heights,* and the motive of Emily Brontë, which constitutes one of the threads of the "biographies" of Dickinson's words and poetry, is itself read as the motive of a "doomed defiant oneness of Heathcliff and Catherine" (62), of a "complete union with another soul . . . Catherine and Heathcliff are each other's central source. They contain, define, and defy one another, and everyone else around them" (136). Relational identity is thus mirrored several times in Howe's text: Howe's relational text constructs Dickinson's poem which, in its turn, both articulates relation and is also itself relational to Emily Brontë's novel. This novel, again, is a novel about a "doomed defiant oneness," or a specific relation, of two beings.

The relation of analogy (repetition of "my") between the title of Howe's text (*My Emily Dickinson*) and the opening line of Dickinson's poem, "My Life had stood . . . ," announces the relational identities of the text. Dickinson's poem has a woman/Gun realized (hunting) only after being identified and carried away by the Master. The lines "My Life had stood—a Loaded Gun— / In Corners—till a Day / The Owner passed—identified— / And carried Me away—" are echoed in Howe's *My Emily Dickinson,* who had been a "loaded but unfired gun" until I (the reader/writer) came along. Just as the woman/Gun is realized through her relation with the other, Emily Dickinson's poem is realized through Susan Howe's reading.

The relational identity of *My Emily Dickinson* reenacts some crucial aspects of "individuality as togetherness" of Vrkljan's *Marina.* A woman's relational identity is made by writing herself that is reading the other. A woman's text is made not by silencing but by giving voice to this other, and the fragmented form of text creates the spaces of contact rather than the narrative of one's "separate" identity. The identity of a poem/woman makes itself as the cross-culturalism of various historical epochs (the past and present of New England) and various readings.

Relational Subjectivity: Empathetic Imagination

Both Vrkljan's and Howe's works articulate woman as a relational identity based on contact with others. This identity is constructed on the level of subjectivity, on one hand, and the level of social practices of relating to other people, on the other hand. In both works, empathy is one basis for relational subjectivity. The extensive research on the "other" provides facts for this empathy, but another important trait of it is imagination: the ability to imagine oneself as another. "Myself was as another, now 'I' dare to go farther," writes Howe in the chapter entitled "To Imagination" (61).

Relational subjectivity as empathetic imagination, going through the other and becoming the other, redefines and reconstitutes our own words and ourselves. In this feminine appropriation of the Hegelian Absolute Spirit coming to itself by going through the other, a woman creates and changes herself through the relation of empathetic identification with the other. Woman as the "unreal reality" of poetry is "connections between unconnected things" (97). The empathetic imagination, being "another," allows change: "I can go farther."

The empathetic imagination which transforms the "I's" subjectivity through the "I's" identifying relation with "you" is a transitive and proliferating one. A "transitive" relation with "you" implies my being related not solely with you, but also with that which relates to "you." As a reading of Dickinson's poem, Howe's text thus also entails its own relation with and constitution of things this poem relates to, such as Victorian New England, Calvinist philosophers, captivity narratives, and so on.

Emily Dickinson was born exactly two hundred years after the Great Migration led by John Winthrop brought her ancestors to America. Like Hawthorne, and unlike Emerson, her conscience still embraced the restless contradictions of this Puritan strain. Her ancestors, rigid Calvinists determined to walk the ancient ways and not to stumble on the path of Righteousness, voluntarily severed themselves from their origins to cross the northern ocean on a religious and utopian errand into the wilderness. Calvinism grounded in the Old Testament, through typological interpretation of the New, was an authoritarian theology that stressed personal salvation through strenuous morality, righteousness over love, and an autocratic governing principle over liberty. (38)

The Puritan consciousness of Jonathan Edwards (1703–1758) shadows and prefigures that of Emily Dickinson. . . . In 1855 Samuel Bowles published Josiah Gilbert Holland's *History of Western Massachusetts*. Both men were close friends of the Dickinson family; Emily Dickinson was particularly close to them. Holland, who knew Edwards' writing well and the influence his thinking had exerted on their region, called him "a metaphysician and theologian second to none in America." In fact Edwards was far more than a ranting Calvinist preacher of hellfire and damnation; he was the most astute and original philosopher to write before the age of James, Peirce, and Santayana. (47–48)[18]

In *Marina*, Vrkljan also creates a "transitive" relation resembling that of *My Emily Dickinson*. Vrkljan's contact with Tsvetaeva implies imagining and making contact with the people Tsvetaeva knew, writers she read, her time and space.

Marina loved Ariadna Scriabin. Ariadna gave birth to a daughter two days before Marina's son Mur was born and sent her a knitted jacket for him in Vshenory. Marina notes in her exercise book: "Now we are equal—she, in 1922 still a girl (sixteen), and I already as I am now. I have a son—she has a daughter. Age—that's all canceled out now."

Ariadna, also a poet, married the Jewish writer David Knut. During the Second World War she was in the French resistance movement. She was killed in 1944 in a battle, when she stumbled upon an ambush. Neither woman survived to see the end of the war. "Now we are equal. . . ." (65–66)

Aside from being transitive, relations in the basis of relational subjectivity are also proliferating. A "proliferating" relation with "you" implies that one specific relation (e.g., I/Vrkljan—you/Tsvetaeva) creates a paradigm for one's relating to others (and for one's self-constitution), which makes possible the creation of numerous other relations of the same type. Thus, the "primary" relation between "I"/Vrkljan and "you"/Tsvetaeva forms a new potentially proliferating principle of relational subjectivity and emphatic self-constitution, and therefore enables the creation of *Marina*'s other self-constituting relations between "I" ("Irena Vrkljan") and "you" of the various people factually unrelated to Marina Tsvetaeva, such as a Chilean poet in exile in Berlin, Croatian painter Stančić, or actress Dora Novak. Relational subjectivity creates the space of "Love's powerful attraction" (*My Emily*, 79), in which numerous distant and irrelevant ("unrelated") people are transformed into the "you's" of my self-constituting direct relation with them.

Transitive and proliferating, the empathetic imagination of relational subjectivity of the "I" of Irena Vrkljan or of Howe's text is connecting me not only with one specific "you" (Marina Tsvetaeva or Emily Dickinson) but also with numerous other people, times, and places. Relational self-constitution of subjectivity transforms these seemingly irrelevant and unrelated others into the relevant "you's" of my direct relation with them.

The imaginative relational self-constitution, or relational subjectivity, is one basis of my connection with the others, and thus one of the ways of forming a community: poetry/woman shapes herself as the "connections between unconnected things" (97). Community cannot exist without one's constituting oneself relationally not only externally and materially but also internally and subjectively, transforming one's subjectivity through one's relations with others.

"Material" Practices of Relating
Marina's "Real-Life" Social Relations

In both Vrkljan's and Howe's works, relational identity is constructed not only on the level of subjectivity but also on the level of material practices of relating, such as Howe's text versus its "object" (Emily Dickinson's poem) or *Marina*'s characters in their "real-life" relations. The emphasis on these material practices of relating—rather than on relating as only a matter of subjectivity—is clear in Vrkljan's text: the focus of *Marina* is Marina Tsvetaeva and her relations with others, and not her poetry. Tsvetaeva's and others' writings are employed only if they biographically relate to Tsvetaeva.

> I am always offended when people say that you are a significant poet, and I get most offended when they say that you are a "genius." . . . In front of you, Marina, in front of that what you are, all your verses are such a minute thing, such a crumb. . . . It is sometimes funny to me when they call you a poet. As if there is no more elevated word from that one.[19]

Sonya says these words in Tsvetaeva's own prose work about a woman she herself loved, the Russian actress Sonya Holliday. Vrkljan's work about Tsvetaeva echoes Sonya's words to the same beloved woman.

Tsvetaeva is greater than her poetry because her "poetry" is not limited only to her writings. Vrkljan sees all of Tsvetaeva's relations with others as "poetic," as realizations—in practice which includes but is not limited to writing—of transformative and unique ways of being together. Tsvetaeva's individuality as "togetherness" is created through her relations with others (with her husband, Sergei, and her children, the poets Rilke and Pasternak, the painter Natalia Goncharova, or the poet Ariadna Scriabin), in which this "other" enacts the possibility of "my" realization, freedom, and change, and in which "I" say myself by voicing the others.

Embedded in the traditional modes of interpersonal relations—correspondence with Rainer Maria Rilke or Boris Pasternak, marriage with Sergei, mothering, friendships, and love affairs—Tsvetaeva's relations with others are unique and challenging in ways that are difficult to name. Vrkljan does not name or interpret Tsvetaeva's relations with others but rather only narrates them by creating her own text or by using other people's biographical reminiscences of Tsvetaeva. The naming or interpretation of these relations would reduce their uniqueness to a comparison with that which is already known and familiar: "There are no comparisons. *That* is life" (*Marina,* 111).

Two years later, towards the end of December 1929 Marina met the painter Natalia Goncharova.

Paris, a café, grayness behind the glass. Two women sit opposite one another for the first time. The bony, tall Goncharova, whom Marina was to love at once. Partly because of the name of Pushkin's wife. Marina would go to the studio and soon begin her first long text about painting. After all, there were paintings as well, Marina.

In that text which has never been translated from Russian, Pushkin's wife is always present too—the destinies of the three women intertwine—the Paris sun is present as well, all the colours of Natalia's paintings, her workshop:

I saw the workshop for the first time in daylight. . . . My first Goncharova workshop—the unadulterated image of labour in the sweat of your brow. And beneath the first sun. In such heat it is impossible to eat (it's not worth drinking anything), impossible to sleep, talk, breathe. Only one thing is possible, and that can always be done; always must be done—it is possible to work. And it was not the glass that melted—but the brow.

I remember, that first time, somewhere to one side, some kind of terrace which later disappeared. Beneath it the gables of the roofs—above it one of Goncharova's Paris paintings—vertically above one of her suns—and I beneath it. In my life I had never felt hotter—better. . . . Goncharova's movements—those of a girl from the very heart of things: doing, inventing, creating. The movement of action. The movement of talent. (And of a blow!)   (76–78)

A diary note written by Tsvetaeva's ten-year-old daughter Alya about her mother indirectly articulates Tsvetaeva's relation to her daughter not only by its content but even more by its formal characteristics. The perceptiveness, vocabulary, language, strikingly skillful writing, and intellectual independence present in Alya's note all shed light on her upbringing and implicit relation with her mother:

My mother is very strange. . . . She is sad, quick, and loves Poems and Music. She writes poems. She is patient and tolerant in the extreme. Even when she's angry she is loving. She is always in a hurry. She has a big heart. A gentle voice. A quick step. Her fingers are full of rings. Marina reads at night. (90)

Marina depicts Tsvetaeva's relations with others that are always those of love and, in a more mundane register, those outside the sphere of direct political practice. However, precisely these "poetic" relations become those of the firmest existential support and daring political stance. In exile in Prague and Paris in the 1930s, Tsvetaeva's family literally lives off her friends. In the long years after Tsvetaeva's suicide in 1941, one of these friends still in Russia, Boris Pasternak, will be writing letters and sending books to Tsvetaeva's daughter Alya, exiled to Siberia.

Tsvetaeva's relations of love create a community with some potential to withstand or oppose the political system. Also, these "poetic" material practices of interpersonal relations make a space of many narratives, irreducible to one principle, that tell of the ways of being together different from those promoted by the systems of power, be they in Tsvetaeva's Russia or in Vrkljan's Yugoslavia or West Germany. The narratives of these personal relations tell of the ways of being together that by themselves show what is wrong with the systems to be and that are today lacking not because of the absence of people or material means, but because of the absence of poetic imagination, which could envision what relations with others could be in the first place. "In front of you, Marina, in front of that what you are, all your verses are such a minute thing, such a crumb. . . ."

Feminine "Mastery": The Relation of Howe's Text to Dickinson's Poem

While Vrkljan exposes the "poetic" quality of Tsvetaeva's real-life social relations, Howe, in opposition to the abundance of biographical writing in the United States, focuses not on Emily Dickinson's life (though she gives references to it) but rather on a Dickinson poem. The "poetry's" articulation of relating between "I" and the other is derived from this poem itself, as well as from many literary references whose echoes Howe's text finds in this poem.

> The subject and conflict of *Wuthering Heights* and "My Life had stood—a Loaded Gun—" is complete union with another soul and absolute separation. Catherine and Heathcliff are each other's central source. They contain, define, and defy one another, and everyone else around them. In Dickinson's poem, this same unity is at the core of identity—Gun and hunter, My and Master. (*My Emily*, 136)

Howe's reading explicates this "unity at the core of identity" or this relating between "I"/a woman/loaded Gun and the "Master"—a relating that realizes My/woman's life or "fires" a Loaded Gun/My life—as (among other things) envy and emulation, slavery, emancipation and eroticism, power, conversion, and death.

> Love, a binding force, is both envy and emulation. (117)

> This austere poem is the aggressive exploration by a single Yankee woman, of the unsaid words—slavery, emancipation, and eroticism. (129)

> Conversion is a sort of Death, a falling into Love's powerful attraction. Power is pitiless once you have put it on. (79)

The relation between "I" and "you" in Dickinson's poem or love as the "unity at the core of identity" makes itself on the basis of recognizable modes of power relations, eroticism, and conversion as death. Reading and writing Dickinson's poem, *My Emily Dickinson* also brings about pain, submission, and sadism as some of the aspects of relating and self-constitution.

> Sadism knocks down barriers between an isolate soul and others. Violence forces reaction. That unity of souls may be linked to sadism is the sad riddle of the world. (136)

On the one hand, statements such as the ones above display a truly ingenious understanding, from one poet to another, of the zone of meanings and the drift of Dickinson's poem, verbalizing as they do some of the disturbing insights derived from this poem, like the one about the link between the unity of souls and violence or sadism. On the other hand, however, these same statements might have the impact of reducing the uniqueness of Dickinson's poem by translating it into already known "truths" about love as conversion, death, power, or sadism. In other words, if Dickinson's poem were primarily marking slavery, sadism, and so on, as the aspects of self-constituting relation with the other, it might not be doing anything so very unique or transformative for the readers of the post-Freudian age. Howe's text repeatedly claims that Dickinson's poem does much more than reiterate commonly known truisms; this surplus, however, is to an extent dissolved by a reading of the "I-you" relation in Dickinson's poem as an increasingly recognizable one (power, emancipation, and so forth). By interpreting Dickinson's poem through the general truisms of love's "power and death," Howe's text displays its own relation toward Dickinson's poem as one which, paradoxically, dissolves the uniqueness of this poem at the same time at which it asserts it.

Another aspect of *My Emily Dickinson*'s dissolution of the individuality of that which the text relates to (Dickinson's poem) is enacted by the overemphasized "transitiveness" of this relation. Namely, Howe's text relates itself to Dickinson's poem, which is, in turn, constructed as relating to Dickinson's historical context and her readings (e.g., Shakespeare, Emily Brontë, Browning, and so on). The overemphasized "transitiveness" of the relation between Howe's text and Dickinson's poem lies in the dissolution of the poem into the things the poem is constructed as relating to.

Dickinson's poem becomes an "echo" of the texts and contexts it is related to: the unique response of the poem to its predecessors and contemporaries is repeatedly announced[20] but not always articulated. Instead, the poem is often reduced to and identified with that which it is related to. It is torn apart by the centrifugal forces of other texts, known facts about women in Victorian New England, general truisms, and so on.

> Shakespeare's four History Chronicles of the Wars of the Roses are formal fast-paced dramas, arranged in a rigidly patterned ceremonial sequence.

During his lifetime they were the most popular of all his plays, but with the exception of *Richard III* they are seldom produced anymore. (85)

"My Life had stood—a Loaded Gun—" is one of Dickinson's most powerful and puzzling poems. The first verse seems to be a direct response to the first verse of "Childe Roland." In the second, she seizes up Browning's indebtedness to Shakespeare's early history plays for his own Dramatic Monologues. (91)

Gun hovers in subjective space, symbol of her own sway. Gun is only a weapon. Without her Master to grip, aim, and pull her trigger, she has no use. Women of Dickinson's class and century, existed in a legal and financial state of dependence on their fathers, brothers, or husbands, that psychologically mutilated them. Excluded from economic competition (hunting), they were forced to settle for passive consumerism. (84)

The relation of the "feminine Ear" of Howe's text toward Dickinson's poem is not fully innocent of the destruction of the uniqueness of this poem. The "feminine Ear" can also be aggressive of the other and can thus resemble a "masculine gaze." The progress of Howe's text (from part 1 to part 6 of Dickinson's poem), or the progress of relating with Dickinson's poem, which is at the basis of Howe's text, is at the same time the process of a dissolution of the poem's uniqueness.

The self-constituting relation of Howe's text with Dickinson's poem thus both creates and at the same time destroys this other (Dickinson's poem). Through its being related to the "generalizing" interpreter (Howe's text), the poem "My Life had stood—a Loaded Gun—" is, in some places, reduced to the speaking of known forces of power or sadism. Through its being related to the texts and contexts it echoes, the poem sometimes gets dissolved into these texts and contexts. The celebrated uniqueness of the poem's response to its influences, and its rearticulation of the general truisms—Dickinson's "gold" which she spun out of the "straw" of her readings and context—is thus often lost.

Vrkljan and Howe on the Closures of Gender: Final Remarks

Relational Feminine Identity: The In-Between Realm

In the dialogue between *Marina or About Biography* and *My Emily Dickinson*, searching for new forms of writing equals searching for new forms of woman's identity. In both texts, the first step of this quest involves efforts to become unique and individual, one's own, through the individualization of one's words. This process removes the words from the group-based and group-given dictionary definitions into the realm of individual meaning and related real-life practices. The meanings of words such as "poetry," "war," "music," "pinecone," "death," and others are created within the context of one specific life. A woman herself makes the meaning of her words, says what "I" or "art" or "death" signify for her, and lives these words accordingly.

The word "woman" itself is thus wrested not only from the patriarchal generic definitions of what a woman is but also from the sometimes generic and generalizing feminist definitions of what a "woman" is or should be. Every woman imagines and reinvents herself in entirely idiosyncratic and individual ways, bound neither by dictionaries of a traditional society nor by those of oppositional feminisms.

The two texts, however, do not stop at this individualization. Individualism wrests a woman and her words from the homogenizing and hegemonic realm of group identity. But individualism also means separateness from the others, isolation and loneliness, enclosure within the boundaries of one's own self, one's own past and imagination. This closure of one's self is articulated through an opposing and liberating reaction of these two texts, a reaction that creates relational—rather than solipsistic—writing and woman's identity. After becoming individual but also alone, a woman next creates her words and autobiography relationally, through contact with other people's different definitions of words and different biographies. Contact with others may affect and change one's own understanding and practice of words and life and is thus a realm of possible freedom from the boundaries of one's own self.

Relational identity presupposes listening to the others and having an emphatic relation with them. The two texts define the very subjectivity of a woman as this emphatic listening of and contact with the others. Relational identity is not loud or self-assertive and does not turn others into the objects of our own speech or practice. The others are seen as subjects in their own right, who interact with me and are of crucial importance for me. Connections with others are in the basis of a woman's identity and poetry. As Howe puts it, poetry is "falling into love's powerful attraction" and "connectedness among unconnected things."

The awareness of relational identity may affect the ways in which we under-stand the process of reading. For example, some contemporary criticism focuses on the ways in which literary works construct gender (for instance, by looking at the construction of women characters), or a specific ethnic or national group. This kind of criticism presupposes a somewhat literal reading: women characters in the work are the only women created by this work. What happens, however, if the process of reading, based on relational identity, works on a level different from this literal one? What if I, a woman, relate to the male characters of the novel equally or sometimes even more so than to the female ones, thus finding myself, say, more in Charles than in Sarah when reading John Fowles's *The French Lieutenant's Woman*, or more in the Master than in Margarita when reading Bulgakov's *Master and Margarita*?

I, a woman, might be fully inclusive—rather than exclusive—not only of male characters but also of all the "formal" characteristics of a text, such as the particularities of the language, the intelligence and humor present in it, this work in its entirety. Consequently, the "woman" of that specific literary work is present not only in female characters but also in many other aspects of the work that contribute to the creation of a woman—the woman that a reader becomes through contact with it all. Looking primarily at the literal level of the construction of female characters, some gender criticism thus asks a reader to change her focus of vision from the background of what is created by the entire text to the foreground of the recognizable motives, and to switch from reading based on the relational and metaphoric identity (I=all) to reading based on the more exclusive and nonrelational identity.

Described in different ways but always assuming an opposition to "masculine" assertiveness, talking, and objectification of others, relational identity has been seen as positive by much of the feminist theory. But a dialogue between Vrkljan's and Howe's works shows that relational identity has both good and bad sides. It is good, among other things, because it provides one means of cohesion within the community. Namely, if people's identities were more substantially relational, based on an empathy with others and changed through the contact with others, then connections among people would not be mechanical and external ones but rather intimate and subjective ties forged within a person.

However, relational emphatic identity can also be destructive and self-destructive. It can dissolve itself into the people and things it relates to, destroying its own specificity and literally merging itself with the others, and thus losing its own individuality. The "I" of Vrkljan's later piece, *Dora, This Autumn* (1991), is fully lost in the "I" of another person, actress Dora Novak, and does not retain any traits of its own separate identity. In a similar way, Howe's text's emphasis on the relations between Dickinson's poem "My Life had stood . . ." and its various historical and literary contexts dissolves this poem into these relations and things the poem relates to, and thus destroys to an extent its separateness and uniqueness. Relational identity, which is a liberating response to the closures of an individual's isolation, can thus itself become a closure.

Both Vrkljan's and Howe's texts make an experiment. They take to the extreme an often repeated call for the identity (usually seen as feminine) that is sympathetic to others and considerate of others, which is based, in its innermost core, on relations with others. They show that this presumably ideal identity could be as destructive and self-destructive as the ones it tries to oppose, that the "feminine" sympathetic ear can be as dangerous as the "masculine" self-assertive speech.

The simple replacement of talking with listening, of isolation with connectedness with others, and of self-centeredness with empathy is not the solution. The solution, this dialogue indicates, lies in the realm in between. In this realm, the closure of one's self is balanced by connections with the others, but this connectedness is, in its turn, balanced by self-centeredness, by the "I's" withdrawing from the others into its own unique creations of life and/or of poetry. This in-between realm is a precious balance, negotiated anew for every different context and every different moment.

Poetry as an Art of Social Relations

In this dialogue, the sought-after feminine identity not only is envisioned as internalized and subjective, as identity discernible mainly in the works of poetry and autobiographical writing. This identity also appears in real-life relations with other people. These relations, in turn, can be shaped by the poetic imagination in the same way in which texts and poetry can be shaped. In Vrkljan's text, Marina Tsvetaeva's poetry is not only—or even primarily—found in her poems; it is rather in her ways of living her life and being with the others. A dialogue on gender sees such unique ways of living as generally absent, not because they are oppressed or not allowed, but because of the lack of poetic imagination necessary to envision them. It is this lack of poetic imagination that is pointed out as the crucial closure preventing the creation of new forms of living and identity.

This imagined literary dialogue sees poetry and the poetic imagination as a creative force shaping one's overall being. In other words, poetry should spill out from the mere writing of texts into real life. As Vrkljan puts it in one of her latter works,

> Sometimes it is conversations with friends [that are also writing], although there are no papers anywhere. It is always also about the "drowned" poems, "drowned" only apparently, because they are not published. . . . It is a collective book, anyway. . . . Thus art is also in being together with the others; the association of that which is un-written should be in balance with that which is written.[21]

"Art is also in being together with the others." The imagination that we customarily give to art and poetry should also be shaping our social relations as well. Poetry should create our social life and our social life should itself become poetry. What is unwritten should balance what is written. A book we need is not only something we write and read but something we live.

Ultimately, a dialogue on gender articulates as a closure the containment of poetry within the covers of one's book and one's work. The primacy of writing and work is exposed and challenged. The sought-after woman's identity implies poetry that can be seen not only as a collection of poems but also as the creator and shaping force of life in all its aspects. This dialogue on gender therefore envisions the feminist project as primarily a poetic one; it involves the awareness of immense possibilities of poetry turned into life.

A woman can attempt to find herself not solely by becoming aware of the ways in which she is oppressed by or objectified in a patriarchal society, or by making herself into the opposite of the masculine other. These projects, traditionally dominant in feminist endeavors, can only go so far. An endeavor to forge new ways of existence, like poetry, leads to "transfiguration beyond gender" (*My Emily*, 138) to the realms where the feminist project becomes a broadly humanist one. In these realms, woman cannot shed modes of identity that stifle one's human and creative potentials only by being aware that these modes are degrading and limiting. But the explosive potentials of poetry could do the trick. As Susan Howe puts it, "[p]oetry is the great stimulation of life" (138). Poetry—and literature in general—can envision a life and identity that are so radically different from existent ones that they might create an impetus to change.

Afterword

Dialogues and the Freedom of Reading

Some years ago, when I tried to explain to one of my acquaintances why I find John Cage's work so fascinating, he abruptly interrupted me with the words: "You cannot just read Cage in any odd way; you cannot even begin to understand what he is about without first studying the American and European avant-garde, the nature of his collaboration with Merce Cunningham, Cage's indebtedness to Suzuki, Thoreau, and a host of other intellectual figures, post–World War II American history." My companion went on to tell me all the many things I should know in order to approach Cage's work properly. I was only too happy to familiarize myself with some of the things on my colleague's list, but it was the prohibitive "you cannot" from his speech that has bothered me ever since.

What are the proper contexts and the "right" ways of reading a literary work? Is there one such way, or a few, or many? Who tells us how to read a book, and why do we listen? As I mention in the introduction to this book, it is obvious that a literary work is part of its time and space, national literary traditions, poetic realms, and so on, but it is also a part of other times and spaces, both in its genesis and its sphere of influence. When it is made, a literary work collects, like a prism, a myriad of idiosyncratically selected elements coming from various times and places and being uniquely transformed through a creative process, giving birth to something new. When it is read, a literary work again functions as a prism whose rays reach out into various times and places, conversing with everyone who reads it. It is this delocalized and homeless (yet at home everywhere) agency of a literary work that has interested me the most in the creation of the imagined literary dialogues that form this book.

If a literary work is indeed literary—regardless of how we may define this literary quality—then literature itself should be one of its most self-evident fields of contextualization and understanding. Moreover, this literature does not have to be divided along national or historic boundaries. These groupings can certainly inform us, but they severely restrict the potentials of our reading. As Cage would put it, interpenetrations are always here, and we do not have to reduce and simplify them to the schemes of relations from our heads. When two tones are put together, they cannot fail to produce a certain relation, and something similar may happen when two otherwise "unrelated" literary works are allowed to enter into a dialogue in a reading that creates that dialogue.

How can we acknowledge the agency and freedom of a creative act that cannot be reduced to its historical context, recognizable political values, or theoretical concepts, and that is potent not only in its day and age and for its immanent audience but also for different times and readers as well? How can we articulate new realms made by literary works rather than translate a novelty into known conceptual frames? Aside from creating literary dialogues, my book also attempts to show that we can read literature without knowing in advance what we are actually looking for (for example, this or that historical or political feature) and also without seeing literature through the lenses of strong literary theories, which thus take the role of the primary discourse.

Rather than applying the established notions of, say, what is progressive and what is reactionary to literature, the three literary dialogues in this book try to find what literary works themselves articulate as closures and liberating practices of language, power, and gender. As Erich Auerbach says at the end of his endlessly inspiring study *Mimesis:*

> My interpretations are no doubt guided by a specific purpose. Yet this purpose assumed form only as I went along, playing as it were with my texts, and for long stretches of my way I have been guided only by the texts themselves.[1]

At its conclusion, *Imagined Dialogues* also poses some new questions. If the liberating potential of literature can be activated only in the act of reading, individually by each and every reader, how can we cultivate such a reading that is able to sense unpredictable novelty and is not intimidated from following its own idiosyncratic paths in an encounter with a literary work?

The reading of literature should be as free as the writing of it. This reading creates its own laws, its own consistency and coherence; it should answer to itself but not to some externally given criteria of what is right and wrong, and it should not doubt itself because voices of authority say that one cannot possibly understand a literary work unless one approaches it in this or that accepted way of which this authority itself happens to be the master.

Such reading should also be free to create connections among "factually" un-related literary works. The dialogues in this book make three specific connections between one Eastern European and one American or English literary work; they also point at a huge realm of the so far unexplored "imagined dialogues" among usually unrelated literary works. The creation of imagined dialogues can enrich us immensely. It can provide us, the readers who make these conversations, with the best interlocutors we can ever hope to find; it can help us to get out of our own ways of seeing the world and therefore enlarge our potentials of both thinking and acting differently, or recognize or confirm our own thoughts or actions.

Such dialogical readings reveal a vast realm of previously unseen connections among writings and people from different places and different times. We can read literary works from these "other" places and times the way we have always read them: not only to find what they can tell us about others but also to find what they can tell us about ourselves, what "news from the inmost being" they bring to us who may become ever so slightly different in the process of reading, to us who share much with the others who wrote these books, to us who can begin to include these others in the very concept of "us."[2] With the help of such reading, we may be enabled to move forward and realize potentials that we were not aware of before.

Notes

Introduction

1. Program notes from a lecture delivered by John Fowles, Fifth Avenue Theater, Seattle, April 22, 1996.

2. This and other examples quoted in my introduction come from the following haphazardly chosen catalogs: Columbia University Press "Literary and Cultural Studies" 1997 catalog, Princeton University Press 1996 sale catalog, University of Pennsylvania Press 1997 literary catalog, and Routledge "Literary and Cultural Studies" 1997 catalog.

3. Mary Louise Pratt, "Scratches on the Face of the Country; or, What Mr. Barrow Saw in the Land of the Bushmen," in *"Race," Writing and Difference*, ed. Henry Louis Gates, Jr. (Chicago: University of Chicago Press, 1986), 144.

4. Ernst Bloch et al., *Aesthetics and Politics*, trans. and ed. Ronald Taylor (London: NLB, 1977), 97.

5. Such political criticism exhibits some rather disturbing resemblances of the much more literal-minded practices of socialist realism, in which "progressive" meant, for example, literature's didactic pointing out of workers' oppression in a capitalist society, the rise of working class consciousness, and the path toward the proletarian revolution. Literary texts that clearly exhibited progressive agenda were good; the other ones were bad.

6. Witold Gombrowicz, *Diary*, vol. 1, trans. Lillian Vallee (Evanston: Northwestern University Press, 1988), 29.

7. Ibid., 22.

8. One can defend political criticism by saying that, for instance, even though Ernest Hemingway's writings might seem misogynist, we can still consider them to be great. The problem, however, lies precisely in the fact that this "great" writing is left mostly unaccounted for in political readings. What makes a literary work great if it is "politically bad"? Does this great writing perhaps transform the "badness" into something entirely different from what it would be outside of the literary work, something so different that it makes little sense to speak of it as still "bad"? Are Jane Austen's novels bad because they do not bother to look beyond the world of the comfortable English gentry and see, for example, all those servants employed in great houses and all those peasants working for the gentry? Is her *Mansfield Park* bad because it hardly asks a question about what

exactly are those affairs in the West Indies that keep the master of the house, Sir Thomas Bertram, away for so long from his family and children, who, in the meantime, are fully occupied—as is the novel itself—with their sentimental activities?

9. This anecdote is found in Ernesto Grassi's book *Moć mašte* (*The Power of Imagination*), trans. Maja Hausler (Zagreb, Croatia: Školska knjiga, 1981), 24.

10. These quotes are taken from papers presented at the Twenty-fifth Annual Twentieth-Century Literature Conference, University of Louisville, February 1997.

11. One reader of this manuscript reminded me that the term "closure" already has a specific meaning in literary criticism (where it denotes a way an author brings a work to its end) and suggested that I try to find another name for my concept. After trying out various alternative possibilities (such as "ideologem" or "mold," for instance), I decided to stick with my first choice. As imperfect as it is because of the above concern, the term "closure" is still the best I could find for expressing the negative quality—of enclosing the human mind and practice—without at the same time putting forth any positive definition of what this enclosing is about so that we have to discover anew in every particular instance, with the help of literature, what it is exactly that constitutes a given "closure."

12. John Cage, *Silence* (Middletown, Conn.: Wesleyan University Press, 1961; reprint, Middletown, Conn.: Wesleyan Paperback, 1973), 100 (page citations are to the reprint edition).

Encountering at times some historical issues, my book also attempts a somewhat different reading from the one currently dominant in historical literary research. Instead of looking for and identifying a relation between specific historical events or already known historical processes on one hand and literary works on the other, I try to see how literary texts themselves point at the so far unperceived aspects of historical fabrics.

Danilo Kiš's stories, for example, would make us think that specific ways of the public use of language—such as the ironic one—are some of the aspects of history that are immensely important yet rarely taken into account. (While I start discussions of Danilo Kiš's and Irena Vrkljan's works with regard to their articulation of a few aspects of their historical contexts, I am more interested in trying to see how these works deal with the more generally present problems of language and gender. And the one context this book makes for Cage's *Silence* or Susan Howe's *My Emily Dickinson* is primarily the one of their dialogues with Eastern European counterparts and not that of their local historical conditions.)

13. Milan Kundera, *Testaments Betrayed*, trans. Linda Asher (New York: HarperCollins, 1995), 14.

14. Gary Saul Morson and Caryl Emerson, *Mikhail Bakhtin: Creation of a Prosaics* (Stanford: Stanford University Press, 1990), 55.

1   Literature against the Closures of Language

1. Brooke Horvath, "Danilo Kiš: An Introduction," *The Review of Contemporary Fiction* 14, no. 1 (spring 1994): 97.

2. Ibid.

3. These are the words of Kiš's acquaintance, writer Pavle Djonović, quoted in Radovan Jablan's "Danilo Kiš izbliza" ("Danilo Kiš from a Close Distance"), *Stvaranje: Časopis za književnost i kulturu* 45, no. 10 (October 1990): 1088.

4. See Boro Krivokapić, ed., *Treba li spaliti Kiša? (Should Kiš Be Burned?)* (Zagreb, Croatia: Globus, 1980); and Serge Shishkoff, "Košava in a Coffee Pot, or a Dissection of a Literary *cause célèbre,*" *Cross Currents* 6 (1987): 341–71. The Yugoslav literary establishment divided itself over Kiš, as he had some prominent intellectuals (e.g., Predrag Matvejević of Zagreb University) "fighting" on his side as well. In his "Faction or Fiction in *A Tomb for Boris Davidovich:* The Literary Affair" (*The Review of Contemporary Fiction* 14, no. 1 [spring 1994]: 169), Vasa D. Mihailovich asserts that

> [n]o other literary affair in postwar [post–World War II] Yugoslav literature
> has aroused so much interest and passion. . . . The affair dogged Kiš for the
> rest of his life, and it is an intelligent guess that it contributed indirectly to
> his early death.

The literary establishment accused Kiš of plagiarism; in this ridiculous slur, Mihailovich finds "a simple jealousy among Kiš's peers," "mutual intolerance toward different literary views," and "intolerance of different political views" (169–70).

5. Joseph Brodsky, introduction to *A Tomb for Boris Davidovich,* by Danilo Kiš (New York: Penguin Books, 1980), xii; subsequently cited as *Tomb.*

6. Danilo Kiš, "Entretien avec Danilo Kiš," interview by Norbert Czarny, *La Quinzaine Littéraire* 447 (September 16–30, 1985): 17.

7. Dragan Klaić, "Danilo Kiš: The Theatrical Connection," *The Review of Contemporary Fiction* 14, no. 1 (spring 1994): 204.

8. Ibid., 207. For Clifford's notion of the identity that is conjunctural rather than authentic, see James Clifford, *The Predicament of Culture* (Cambridge, Mass.: Harvard University Press, 1988), especially the introduction.

9. Danilo Kiš, "Tražim mesto pod suncem za sumnju" ("I Am Looking for a Place under the Sun to Put Doubt"), *Izraz* 68, no. 9 (September 1990): 202.

10. Ibid., 198–99.

11. John Cage, "Here Comes Everybody: Overpopulation and Art," lecture given at Stanford University, January 28, 1992. Subsequently published as "Overpopulation and Art," in *John Cage: Composed in America,* ed. Marjorie Perloff and

Charles Junkerman (Chicago: University of Chicago Press, 1994), 21. (The exact quotation in a published verison is: "a world wiThout art / and that wasn't bad.")

12. Richard Kostelanetz, *Conversing with Cage* (New York: Limelight Editions, 1991), 212.

13. Ibid., 216.

14. Ibid., 233.

15. Ibid., 221.

16. Danilo Kiš, "A Tomb for Boris Davidovich," in *A Tomb for Boris Davidovich*, 73.

17. Refuting accusations of plagiarism charged against him, Kiš himself wrote about changing this brief anecdote taken from Steiner's memoir by expanding it into an entire story, previously absent. Danilo Kiš, *Čas anatomije* (*The Anatomy Lesson*) (Belgrade, Yugoslavia: Nolit, 1978), 215.

18. Kiš's project in *A Tomb for Boris Davidovich* greatly resembles the project of another "Eastern European" writer, East German Christa Wolf, in her novel *Cassandra* (1983). This novel is reclaiming the "lost text" of Cassandra's thoughts on the afternoon before her execution. While approaching Agamemnon's palace, where she will be executed, Cassandra recalls in great detail the genesis of the war between Troy and Greece, and the predicament of the individual in the war. The prophetess has acquired the knowledge of the war and is aware that this dearly paid wisdom would greatly benefit future generations and perhaps help them to avoid repeating the mistakes of Cassandra's time. That is why Cassandra wishes to stay alive just in order to share her wisdom with "a scribe, or better yet a young slave woman with a keen memory and a powerful voice," who would start the oral passage of Cassandra's words to "those faraway, perhaps happier people who will live in times to come" (Christa Wolf, *Cassandra*, trans. Jan van Heurck [New York: Farrar, Straus and Giroux, 1988], 81). Cassandra does not stay alive. However, her question "What I grasp between now and evening will perish with me. Will it perish?" (5) is answered negatively by Christa Wolf's novel. A text of what Cassandra "grasped between now and evening" did not perish: the faraway future writer "finds" this text and gives it back to the community that such texts might help to create. On the subject of Kiš's writing missing texts, see also Branko Gorjup, "Textualizing the Past: The Function of Memory and History in Kiš's Fiction," *The Review of Contemporary Fiction* 14, no. 1 (spring 1994): 161–68.

19. See Danilo Kiš, *The Encyclopedia of the Dead*, trans. Michael Henry Heim (New York: Penguin Books, 1991).

20. Christa Wolf, *The Quest for Christa T.*, trans. Christopher Middleton (New York: Farrar, Straus and Giroux, 1979), 23 (italics mine).

21. Danilo Kiš, "Autobiographical Sketch (Short Autobiography)," *The Review of Contemporary Fiction* 14, no. 1 (spring 1994): 117.

22. Karl-Markus Gauss writes about Kiš's "fanatic love towards detail" and his "rigorous ethics of detail." See Karl-Markus Gauss, "Na dnu Panonskog mora: Danilo Kiš" ("On the Bottom of the Panonian Sea: Danilo Kiš"), in *Uništenje Srednje Evrope* (*The Destruction of Central Europe*), trans. Truda Stamać (Zagreb, Croatia: Durieux, 1994), 61, 63.

23. The texture of Kiš's writing in this book resembles that of Kiš's major literary influence, Argentinean short-story writer Jorge Luís Borges. Kiš discussed at length Borges's importance for his own work. See Kiš, *Čas anatomije*, 52. See also Ilan Stavans, "Danilo Kiš in Buenos Aires," *The Review of Contemporary Fiction* 14, no. 1 (spring 1994): 174; and Kiš, "Tražim mesto pod suncem."

24. The complete phrase is "To be a work [of art] means to set up a world," from Martin Heidegger, "The Origin of the Work of Art," in *Poetry, Language, Thought*, trans. Albert Hofstadter (New York: Harper and Row, 1975), 44.

25. Danilo Kiš, *Garden, Ashes*, trans. William J. Hannaher (London: Faber and Faber, 1985), 68–72.

26. Gauss, "Na dnu Panonskog mora," 61. Kiš himself says:

The Bible with its abridged form, and most of all the Old Testament as used by schoolboys is in effect the book which has impressed me the most since my childhood. . . . The God-Creator was for me never a simple metaphor— it is one conviction, not religious but rather aesthetic. (Kiš, "Entretien," 17)

27. Branko Gorjup, "Danilo Kiš: From 'Enchantment' to 'Documentation,'" *Canadian Slavonic Papers* 29, no. 4 (December 1987): 387.

28. Ibid., 391.

29. Kiš, *Čas anatomije*, 112.

30. Ibid., 110.

31. Wolf, *Quest for Christa T.*, 23.

32. Václav Havel, "The Power of the Powerless," trans. Paul Wilson, in *Václav Havel or Living in Truth*, ed. Jan Vladislav (London: Faber and Faber, 1986), 47.

33. Zdena Salivarová, *Summer in Prague*, trans. Marie Winn (New York: Harper and Row, 1973), 18.

34. Ibid., 19.

35. Ibid., 267.

36. Ibid.

37. Although writing about Eastern European Communist societies, Havel makes clear that "living in lie" applies (though in a somewhat different way), to the "West" as well:

In everyone there is some willingness to merge with the anonymous crowd and to flow comfortably along with it down the river of pseudo-life. . . . In highly simplified terms, it could be said that the post-totalitarian system has been built on foundations laid by the historical encounter between dictatorship and the consumer society. Is it not true that the far-reaching adaptability to living in lie and the effortless spread of social auto-totality have some connection with the general unwillingness of consumption-oriented people to sacrifice some material certainties for the sake of their own spiritual and moral integrity? With their willingness to surrender higher values when faced with the trivializing temptations of modern civilization? With their vulnerability to the attractions of mass indifference? And in the end, is not the grayness and the emptiness of life in the post-totalitarian system only an inflated caricature of modern life in general? And do we not in fact stand (although in the external measures of civilization, we are far behind) as a kind of warning to the West, revealing to it its own latent tendencies? (Havel, *Living in Truth*, 54)

Havel's concept of the "attractions of mass indifference" resembles Baudrillard's concept of "devolution" of the masses, although the causes of the "attractions of mass indifference" in Communist Eastern Europe are different from the causes of "devolution" in the capitalist "West" as conceptualized by Baudrillard. "Devolution" is the masses' "strategic resistance" to the system's demand to "constitute ourselves as subjects, to liberate, to express ourselves at any price, to vote, to produce, to decide, to speak, to participate, to play the game." See Jean Baudrillard, *Selected Writings*, ed. Mark Poster (Stanford: Stanford University Press, 1988), 218. In such a system, "the deepest desire is perhaps to give the responsibility for one's desire to someone else . . . a strategy towards others not of appropriation but, on the contrary, of . . . an expulsion of the obligation of being responsible" (215).

38. Salivarová, *Summer in Prague*, 36.

39. Ibid., 155.

40. As Slovenian theorist Slavoj Žižek comments in one interview, this irony is also readily found in the works of Milan Kundera: "Kundera's ideology consisted in discovering . . . this cynical or ironic distance towards power." Vesna Kesić, "Slovenski dan poslije" ("Slovenian Day After"), *Danas* 496 (August 20, 1991): 53.

41. Miklós Haraszti, *The Velvet Prison*, trans. Katalim Stephen Landesmann, with the assistance of Steve Wasserman (New York: A New Republic Book, 1987), 147.

42. Terry Eagleton, "Absolute Ironies: Søren Kierkegaard," in *The Ideology of the Aesthetic* (Oxford: Basil Blackwell, 1990), 174.

43. Ibid., 174.

44. Ibid., 188.

45. Kiš, *Čas anatomije*, 114.

46. See Baudrillard's article "Simulacra and Simulations," in *Selected Writings*.

47. One would be tempted to call this stance a postmodern one were it not for the fact that the ironic attitude toward narration was familiar for many writers of earlier ages and different places, so it is hard to appropriate and label such a stance, without further discussion, as an exclusively postmodernist one.

48. The sources of *A Tomb for Boris Davidovich* are both real and apocryphal.

Many *sources*, real and false, are mentioned; not only journals and magazines, books, chronicles and histories (from the first or second hand), but also names, real and false. . . .

. . . maniacal insisting on a document, witnessing, fact, quote. (Kiš, *Čas anatomije*, 110, 112)

Kiš uses numerous authentic sources with various degrees of factual deformation.

49. Hayden White, "The Value of Narrativity in the Representation of Reality," in *On Narrative*, ed. W. J. T. Mitchell (Chicago: University of Chicago Press, 1981), 7.

50. Ibid., 8.

51. Philosophies of revolution acquired the power and character of myth in a context that is in Kiš's stories marked by the presence of another myth of the time, the fascist one of "earth and blood." From the story "The Magic Card Dealing," Karl Taube, echoing the famous phrase on communism from the *Manifesto of the Communist Party* ("A spectre is haunting Europe—the spectre of Communism"), "warned the world of the danger: 'A phantom stalks through Europe, the phantom of fascism'" (58).

52. Compare the following:

"I heard as if dazed," writes Levin, "the murmur coming from the salon, accompanied by the din of silver utensils like the tinkling of bells, and saw as through a fog the world we had left behind, and which was irretrievably sinking into the past, as into murky water." (83–84)

53. Milivoj Solar, *Mit o avangardi i mit o dekadenciji* (*Myth of the Avant-garde and Myth of Decadence*) (Belgrade, Yugoslavia: Nolit, 1986), 57.

54. Novsky of this period resembles Dr. Karl Taube (of the story "The Magic Card Dealing") in his disillusionment after coming to Moscow in 1935 and finding out that things were very different from expected.

It is also known that in August 1936 he resided in the Caucuses, where he had accompanied his wife, who had become ill. Ungváry stated that it was tuberculosis, while K.S. claims that she was being treated "for nerves." If we accept the latter explanation (and much circumstantial evidence supports it), it points to the hidden and to us unknown spiritual suffering the Taubes experienced during this period. It is difficult to say whether it was a question of disillusionment or a foreboding of the imminent catastrophe. (61)

(See parts of this story called "The Long Walks" and "Between Acts.")
55. Kostelanetz, *Conversing with Cage*, 216.
56. An example of the synchronicity of events in performance is "Musicircus" (not mentioned in *Silence*). "Musicircus" is an event described by Cage as having "as much music as can be played by all those willing to perform without being paid. Loud and soft. Serious and popular. Young and old. Student recitals. Church choirs. Athletics or dance." (Quoted from the program notes of John Cage's visit to Stanford University, January 1992.) The space(s) and time(s) of the performance are given in advance: every performer is assigned a specific space and time. All the performers do their own things, without harmonizing or "making sense" with each other. The event creates the multiplicity of activities that are each "central, original."
57. Kostelanetz, *Conversing with Cage*, 214.
58. The awareness of the possibility of making our language and our practice liberating, horizontal, and democratic could immensely change the ways in which we think about specific phenomena or problems, talk about them, and try to relate to them. Our concepts and their corresponding practice are not fixed in some ideal sphere but rather changeable with regard to a multitude of contingencies of their particular context. For example, being a "progressive" or a "feminist" or a "radical" and so on might mean one thing in one context and a very different thing in another. Rather than one seeing these concepts as defined once and for all, it is the awareness of and interaction with the multiplicity of centers of a dynamic context that should decide the meaning and the practice of these words in any particular situation.

2   Literature against the Closures of Power

1. Jan Walc, "'When the Earth Is No Longer a Dream and Cannot Be Dreamed through to the End,'" *The Polish Review* 32, no. 2 (1987): 181–82.
2. Tadeusz Drewnowski, *Ucieczka z kamiennego świata (o Tadeuszu Borowskim)* (*Escape from the World of Stone* [*on Tadeusz Borowski*]) (Warsaw: Państwowy Instytut Wydawniczy, 1962), 77.
3. Jan Kott, introduction to *This Way for the Gas, Ladies and Gentlemen*, by Tadeusz Borowski (New York: Penguin Books, 1976), 20; subsequently cited as *This Way*.

The stories in the English edition were selected by translator Barbara Vedder from the two collections of Borowski's stories, *Farewell to Maria* and *A World of Stone* (*Pożegnanie z Marią* and *Kamienny świat*), that were published in Poland in 1948. Borowski wrote the first two stories of this edition, "This Way for the Gas, Ladies and Gentlemen" and "A Day at Harmenz," as soon as he and other Dachau prisoners were liberated by the U.S. Seventh Army (on May 1, 1945) and moved to a camp for displaced persons near Munich.

4. Piotr Kuhiwczak, "Beyond Self: A Lesson from the Concentration Camps," *Canadian Review of Comparative Literature/Revue Canadienne de Littérature Comparée* 19, no. 3 (September 1992): 403.

5. In his conversation with Oe Kenzaburo, Ishiguro says:

I was very aware that I had very little knowledge of modern Japan. But still I was writing books set in Japan, or supposedly set in Japan. My very lack of authority and lack of knowledge about Japan, I think, forced me into a position of using my imagination, and also of thinking of myself as a kind of homeless writer. I had no obvious social role, because I wasn't a very English Englishman, and I wasn't a very Japanese Japanese either. (Kazuo Ishiguro and Oe Kenzaburo, "The Novelist in Today's World: A Conversation," *boundary 2: An International Journal of Literature and Culture* 18, no. 3 [fall 1991]: 115)

Talking about his novel *An Artist of the Floating World*, which is set in Japan, Ishiguro discussed the role of positive knowledge and research about Japan in his work:

I did very little research, primarily because research is only of any interest to me in order to check up after I've done something, to make sure I'm not getting anything wildly wrong. I need certain things to be the way they are in my books for the purposes of my themes. . . . That's what I needed, and as far as I was concerned, things in my Japan were going to operate like that. I am not essentially concerned with a realist purpose in writing. I just invent a Japan which serves my needs. And I put that Japan together out of little scraps, out of memories, out of speculation, out of imagination. ("An Interview with Kazuo Ishiguro," by Gregory Mason, *Contemporary Literature* 30, no. 3 [fall 1989]:340–41)

6. Ishiguro's first novel, *A Pale View of Hills*, won the Winifred Holtby Prize, and his second novel, *An Artist of the Floating World*, won the 1986 Whitbread Book of the Year Award. *The Remains of the Day* received the 1989 Booker Prize.

7. Kott, introduction, 22.

8. Ibid.

9. "The People Who Walked On" is the title of one of Borowski's stories.

10. Tadek describes his encounter as follows:

I find Ivan inside a sheltered nook. With his pocket-knife he is carving designs in the bark of a thick piece of wood—squares, love knots, little hearts, Ukrainian patterns. An old, trusted Greek kneels beside him, stuffing something inside his bag. I just catch sight of a white feathered wing and the red beak of a goose before Ivan, seeing me come in, throws his coat over the bag. The lard has melted inside my pocket and there is an ugly stain on my trousers.

"From Mrs Haneczka," I say in a matter-of-fact tone.

"Didn't she send a message? I was supposed to get some eggs."

"She only asked me to thank you for the soap. She liked it very much."

"Good. I happened to buy it last night from a Greek Jew in Canada. Gave him three eggs for it."

Ivan unwraps the lard. It is squashed, soft and yellowish. The very sight of it makes me nauseous, perhaps because I ate too much smoked bacon this morning, and keep tasting it in my mouth.

"Ah, the bitch! Two such fine pieces of soap and this is all she sends? Didn't she give you any cake?" Ivan looks at me suspiciously.

"You're entirely right, Ivan, she didn't give you enough, that's a fact. I've seen the soap. . . ."

"You have?" He fidgets uneasily. "Well, I must be going. It's time I gave my men a little shove."

"Yes, I saw it. She really has given you too little. You deserve more. Especially from me. And you'll get it, I promise you . . ."

We look hard into each other's eyes. (63–64)

11. Francis Fukuyama, *The End of History and the Last Man* (New York: Avon Books, 1993), 248.

12. "A Day at Harmenz" does not formulate Tadek's rarely mentioned intentions as his (the narrator's) thoughts but rather as an external, material reality. When Tadek gives his second bowl of soup to Andrei in order to get apples in exchange, he does not narrate the action in terms of his motivation or planning but rather translates his intentions into the pure certainty of future reality: "I give my second bowl to Andrei. In return he will bring me apples. He works in an orchard" (70). The same externalizing or materializing of Tadek's thoughts is present in the appearance of his few speculations in the form of spoken dialogues. "'I feel as if this damn selection were somehow my fault. What a curious power words have . . . Here in Auschwitz even evil words seem to materialize'" (80). A spoken dialogue instead of an internal monologue characterizes Tadek's turning toward the outside,

the external world and the other people. But even when employed in a dialogue, speculation is a noneconomical and potentially distracting mode of being. Tadek's interlocutor wisely reminds him that the camp is not the place for speculations but only for ceaseless "realistic" action: " '[T]ake it easy,' said Kazik. 'Instead, let me have something to go with this sausage' " (80).

13. Practical identity is the one largely deprived of individual's personal or cultural idiosyncrasies. While recent literary and cultural studies criticism has emphasized the subversive effects of the inclusion of cultural and other differences in the various power realms, this literary dialogue implies that these subversive effects have been overestimated because various cultural and identity differences do not subvert realities of survival politics. The inclusion of cultural differences provides only an acceptable variation in functioning of a given element of a power system. These differences do not change a power system nor mitigate its ultimately homogenizing effects. When one needs to survive in a given environment, one's practical identity obliterates one's cultural and other differences.

14. Russian literary theorist Mikhail Bakhtin discusses how, for example, the genre of Menipean satire is one of the main creators of a dialogic or polyphonic nature of Dostoevski's novels. Ernesto Laclau and Chantal Mouffe (*Hegemony and Socialist Strategy* [New York: Verso, 1985]), among others, have linked discursive practices of creating the text with the material practices of being in the world.

> The main consequence of a break with the discursive/extra-discursive dichotomy is . . . a major enlargement of the field of those categories which can account for social relations. Synonymy, metonymy, metaphor are not forms of thought that add a second sense to a primary, constitutive literality of social relations; instead, they are part of the primary terrain itself in which the social is constituted. (110)

15. The original title of this story is "U nas, w Auschwitzu." The more literal translation of this title would be something like "In our place, in Auschwitz." Vedder's translation adds the words "home" and "letter," which are not in the original.

16. Tadek's epistolary story includes the genres of storytelling, essay, travelogue (Tadek keeps on making "sightseeing tours" (111), after which he writes descriptions of a "new place" and its inhabitants), and autobiography.

17. Tadek records a "surplus" not only of his own stories (about himself other than in the present moment) but also of the other inmates' stories. These inserted narratives dissolve the unity of an ever-receding main plot (Tadek's medical training in Auschwitz) and stand relatively separate from each other, on their own, as fairly self-sufficient facets of the camp's being. Tadek's stories thematize the various aspects of camps, not only the camp's main function but also different features

of the camps of the "living," people like Tadek himself. He records horrible events with an eye to their grotesque aspect, like the "black humor" story about Tadek's lowering the camp's mortality rate (100), or the following story about Moise's getting some new pictures of his family:

"What's the trouble, Moise?" I said. "You seem out of sorts." "I've got some new pictures of my family." "That's good! Why should it upset you?" "Good? Hell! I've sent my own father to the oven!" "Impossible!" "Possible, because I have. He came with a transport, and saw me in front of the gas chamber. I was lining up the people. He threw his arms around me, and began kissing me and asking, what's going to happen. He told me he was hungry because they'd been riding for two days without any food. But right away the *Kommandoführer* yells at me not to stand around, to get back at work. What was I to do? 'Go on, father,' I said, 'wash yourself in the bath-house and then we'll talk. Can't you see I'm busy now?' So my father went on to the gas chamber. And later I found the pictures in his coat pocket. Now tell me, what's so good about my having the pictures?"
We laughed. (128)

Tadek's fiancée can also read in his letters about the attitude of the camp's inmates toward those destined to be exterminated, as in the story about Tadek and the other ten thousand men standing still and silent while the three vans of women to be gassed, pleading for help, slowly passed them by (116). Included in Tadek's letters, however, are also humorous stories, such as the ones about a marriage in Auschwitz, visits to the "Puff" (brothel section), a boxing match, and a concert.

Secondly—the wedding of the Spaniard. The Spaniard fought defending Madrid, then escaped to France and ended up at Auschwitz. He had found himself a Frenchwoman, as a Spaniard would, and had had a child by her. The child grew. The Spaniard stayed on and on behind the barbed-wire. So the Frenchwoman started clamouring for a wedding. Out goes a petition to H. himself. H. is indignant: "Is there no *Ordnung* in the new Europe? Marry them immediately!"
So they shipped the Frenchwoman, together with the child, to the camp, hurriedly pulled the stripes off the Spaniard's back, fitted him into an elegant suit pressed personally by the Kapo in the laundry room, carefully selected a tie and matching socks from the camp's abundant supplies, and married them.
Then the newlyweds went to have their pictures taken: she with the child at her side and a bouquet of hyacinths in her arms, he standing close to her on the other side. Behind them—the orchestra *in corpore* . . .

The newlyweds, meanwhile, had finished the picture-taking ceremony and were sent to a Puff suite for their wedding night. The regular Puff residents were temporarily exiled to Block 10. The following day the French-woman returned to France, and the Spaniard, again in his stripes, returned to a labour Kommando.

But now everyone at the camp walks proudly, head high.

"We even have weddings in Auschwitz." (134–35)

In the practice-articulating story, "A Day at Harmenz," the relevant and recorded space and time are only the functional space and time of the actual action. But the "now and here" of "A Day at Harmenz" is replaced by a surplus of time and space in "Auschwitz, Our Home," a surplus brought by the mentioning of past, imagining of future, and talking about other places. In his quest for knowledge, Tadek records spaces and times that are not directly connected with his current practice. These "extra" spaces and times may, for example, appear in philosophical excursus in which Tadek condemns slavery in the bases of Egyptian and Greek antiquity, autobiographical reminiscences of the past, and so on.

18. In the reflexive "essayistic" parts of the story, Tadek offers a body of scattered theoretical musings. He asks questions such as, for example, "Why is it that nobody cries out, nobody spits in their faces, nobody jumps at their throats? . . . What is this mystery? This strange power of one man over another? This insane passivity that cannot be overcome?" (112). He also gives a few general answers: for example, he finds hope (that one will ultimately survive) to be one of the main reasons for the above mentioned "insanely" passive behavior, and he also reflects on the fact that misleading camp appearances "suffice to deceive the world—and us" (115). Tadek also defines the right knowledge negatively, as simply being the opposite from the "wrong" knowledge of, for example, Platonic idealism (131) or the Polish Communist Party (137). However, questions about the concentration camps and the war remain largely unanswered in the realm of reflective thinking. Reflective thinking is only one of the many forms of knowledge through which Tadek attempts to understand the camps, rather than the *only* form of knowledge that should homogenize everything in itself.

19. What emerges is a concept that there are numerous ways of knowing through which a phenomenon (such as a concentration camp) should be seen. Not only local historical and political conditions of Germany and Europe of the 1930s are relevant but also Egyptian slavery and Greek thought, not only politics but also aesthetics and religion, not only tragic but also grotesque and endearing, not only storytelling, but also philosophy, prophecy, travel narrative, and letters to the beloved.

Instead of pursuing any of these specific contexts or ways of knowing in a systematic way, knowledge builds itself as a prism of fragments coming from those different areas. Consequently, the knowledge of something that might be a "local phenomenon" is nonlocal itself because it is formed both in relation to faraway phenomena, on one hand, and through modes of speaking (e.g., narrative genres), which are shared with other times and other places, on the other hand. Similarly, the "knowing" identity is not a localized identity of "here and now" (as the practical one) but rather the identity that traverses and draws from a great historical and conceptual span, an identity that is everywhere and thus also nowhere in particular, a "homeless" and delocalized identity. Instead of saying "you cannot know this because you were not here as I was and thus this knowledge is my privilege," this delocalized identity and knowledge would say "I cannot know this without you and the others, because I *know* only through the others and their (our) accumulated and shared ways of knowing."

20. Georg Lukács, *The Theory of the Novel* (Cambridge: MIT Press, 1989), 60, 66.

21. Althusser's concept of "structural causality" poses "causality" not as the relation in which one of the elements is taken to be a determinant cause of other elements but rather as the relation of mediation and interdependency among all the elements. "Structural causality" thus stands for the "entire system of *relationships* among those levels." Fredric Jameson, *The Political Unconscious: Narrative as a Socially Symbolic Act* (Ithaca, New York: Cornell University Press, 1981), 36.

22. In his seminal 1935 essay "The Work of Art in the Age of Mechanical Reproduction," Walter Benjamin characterizes fascism as the aestheticization of politics (in *Illuminations*, trans. Harry Zohn, ed. Hannah Arendt [New York: Schocken Books, 1969]). Discussing Benjamin's notion, Russell Berman talks about the mobilization of aesthetic material "as substitutes for an explicitly political discussion" and maintains that for Benjamin aestheticization is "the central mechanism of fascist politics" (*Modern Culture and Critical Theory: Art, Politics, and the Legacy of the Frankfurt School* [Madison: University of Wisconsin Press, 1989], 32, 73).

Butler Stevens himself articulates the main characteristic of this "aestheticization of politics" in his story about a British butler in India who exhibited the qualities of a perfect professional.

The story was an apparently true one concerning a certain butler who had traveled with his employer to India and served there for many years maintaining amongst the native staff the same high standards he had commanded in England. One afternoon, evidently, this butler had entered the dining room to make sure all was well for dinner, when he noticed a tiger languishing beneath the dining table. The butler had left the dining room quietly, taking care to close the doors behind him, and proceeded calmly to the drawing room where his employer was taking tea with a number of visitors. There he attracted his employer's attention with a polite cough, then whispered in the latter's ear: "I'm very sorry, sir, but there appears to be a tiger in the dining room. Perhaps you will permit the twelve-bores to be used?"

And according to legend, a few minutes later, the employer heard three gun shots. When the butler reappeared in the drawing room some time afterward to refresh the teapots, the employer had inquired if all was well.

"Perfectly fine, thank you, sir," had come the reply. "Dinner will be served at the usual time and I am pleased to say there will be no discernible traces left of the recent occurrence by that time." (36)

The aestheticization of politics is vividly exemplified in this story of "discernible traces" of blood and death erased by the pleasing surfaces of a polished dining room and polite speech—the killing of a tiger is referred to as "perhaps you will permit the twelve-bores to be used?" and a "recent occurrence." During the course of Stevens's narrative, the story of the shot tiger becomes a succinct paradigm of the covering up of death with aesthetic forms. Stevens's father, himself a butler, provides impeccable service to a man referred to as "the General," responsible for the death of Stevens's only brother, when this man visits Mr. Silvers, the employer of Stevens's father. In a perverse balancing act, when Stevens's father (now Darlington Hall's under butler) is himself dying in his small, bleak room, which looks like a "prison cell" (64), Stevens hides this death behind the much more pleasing features that Darlington Hall has to offer (memorable sights of a magnificent banqueting hall and its soft subtle lights) during the 1923 conference. The moment of a symbolic death of Stevens's own potential happiness with Darlington Hall's housekeeper, Miss Kenton, caused by Stevens's refusal to acknowledge his own attachment and leave his professional persona for even a moment, is covered with the pleasing impact of perfectly polished silver during the first meeting between Halifax and Ribbentrop.

23. Stevens's uncritical but "realistic" (allowing his professional survival) practices include the firing of Jewish maids on Lord Darlington's orders, providing spotless dinner service while his own father is dying, and keeping "business as usual" while Miss Kenton is announcing her departure.

24. Features of Stevens's speech enable the creation of his text, which covers up and beautifies his own practice. Caroline Patey identifies and discusses Stevens's rhetorical devices. She talks about the "periphrastic mania (bordering on the metaphorical) [which] is at its best exemplified in the ludicrous episode in which Stevens is asked to tell young Reginald about 'the facts of life.'" See Caroline Patey, "When Ishiguro Visits the West Country: An Essay on *The Remains of the Day*," *Acme: Annali della Facolta di Lettere e Filosofia dell'Universita degli Studi di Milano* 44, no. 2 (May–Aug 1991): 147. She notes that "Stevens' litotes are sometimes so radical as to assume the form of silence" and that he uses understatement to

"mitigate the harshness of reality . . . Lord Darlington's oratorial and diplomatic blunders are referred to as 'a little unfortunate' (p. 98)" (148).

Stevens carefully avoids talking about the war; he focuses his narrative on the events in the 1920s and 1930s and then on the present-day 1950s, alluding to the years of the war only when he cannot omit saying that some character he is talking about has been killed in the war. Thus, mentioning butler Jack Neighbours, for instance, who was "excitedly eulogized" in the midthirties and who very likely held views different from Stevens on the relation between professionalism and politics, Stevens says: "I have nothing against Mr. Jack Neighbours, who sadly, I understand, was killed in the war" (29). Similarly, while reminiscing with Miss Kenton/Mrs. Benn about the past at the end of his journey (and the end of his narrative), and remembering Darlington's young nephew Reginald Cardinal, Stevens was "obliged to go on to inform Miss Kenton of [Reginald Cardinal's] being killed in Belgium during the war" (234).

Preceding this announcement in Stevens's narrative is his recollection of young Cardinal's unsuccessful attempts, in the late 1930s, to persuade Lord Darlington that he was mistaken in supporting the Nazi regime and to alert Stevens to his master's misguided politics. The juxtaposition of past and present shows Darlington's and Stevens's implication in Cardinal's death. It also becomes yet more understandable why Stevens omits any direct talk about the war as much as he can. However, the intense suppression of the topic of the war is strongly felt in Stevens's speech, as many of the events he talks about derive their special meaning from both Stevens's and the readers' awareness of how these events play in the rise of fascism.

3   Literature against the Closures of Gender

1. *Marina or About Biography*'s wealth of information about Tsvetaeva allows one to see this work, among other things, as a piece of poetic biographical scholarship. See Irena Vrkljan, *Marina or About Biography*, trans. Celia Hawkesworth (Zagreb, Croatia: Durieux/The Bridge, 1991); subsequently cited as *Marina*. In turn, Howe postulates that the experimental form of her work (merging between scholarship and poetry) is necessary for the articulation of the radical "shattering . . . of Being" articulated in Dickinson's poem. Howe takes issue here with both Victorian scientists and contemporary feminist literary critics: "Victorian scientists . . . like most contemporary feminist literary critics—eager to discuss the shattering of all hierarchies of Being—didn't want the form they discussed this in to be shattering." See Susan Howe, *My Emily Dickinson* (Berkeley, Calif.: North Atlantic Books, 1985), 116; subsequently cited as *My Emily*.

2. In her "'Collision or Collusion with History': The Narrative Lyric of Susan Howe," Marjorie Perloff writes: "[T]here is not, in any case, so much as a trace in Howe's work of the confessional mode. . . . Except for 'Buffalo. 12.7.41.' in *Pythagorean Silence* (and this only in part), I know of no Howe poem that is directly autobiographical or personal" (*Contemporary Literature* 30, no. 4 [1989]: 519–20).

Given the particular nature of the two texts discussed in this chapter, I chose not to include brief biographies of the two authors in the introduction to the chapter. Vrkljan's works are themselves autobiographies, and the reading of them will show how the author herself writes her life. On the other hand, given the programatically nonautobiographical nature of Howe's *My Emily Dickinson* and her work in general, it seemed inappropriate to say anything more on Howe's life than what we find on the back cover of her book.

Susan Howe is the author of numerous books of poetry, including *The Western Borders, Pythagorean Silence,* and *Defenestration of Prague.* She was the recipient of the American Book Award for poetry from the Before Columbus Foundation in 1981. Born in Boston, Howe now lives with her husband and son in Guilford, Connecticut; she has a grown daughter who is a painter in New York City.

3. This book appeared first in Germany in 1982 under the title *Tochter zwischen Süd und West.* It was published in Croatian in Zagreb in 1984. Vrkljan is bilingual (Croatian and German), and she has been living in West Berlin for half of each year since the late 1960s.

4. As Celia Hawkesworth writes in her discussion of the autobiographical writings of Irena Vrkljan:

Her [Vrkljan's] growing consciousness of her artificial role in this world cannot be separated from a sense of revolt, rejection and a desire to escape. What is both new in Vrkljan's work in the context of Serbian and Croatian literature and at the same time typical of much women's writing of her time is the fact that these emotions are crystallised in anger. ("*Silk, Scissors, Garden, Ashes:* The Autobiographical Writings of Irena Vrkljan and Danilo Kiš," in *Literature and Politics in Eastern Europe: Selected Papers from the Fourth World Congress for Soviet and East European Studies, Harrogate, 1990.* [New York: St. Martin's Press, 1992], 91)

In talking about the absence of gender consciousness in the Yugoslav cultural context, one should qualify this absence by noting the discrepancy between state policies regarding women's issues and society's own gender consciousness. Women in Yugoslavia during the 1980s took for granted policies such as abortion and divorce on demand, paid maternity leave (up to three years), paid family medical leave, gender quota in political bodies, state-supported child day-care facilities, and many others. However, these policies had mostly not been achieved from below, through feminist organizations and grass-roots activity of women themselves, but rather from above, by decrees of the state. One could perhaps speculate that the state's provision of some beneficiary policies with regard to women's issues was one of the reasons for the absence of a more developed gender consciousness among women themselves and within the whole society.

Another reason for this absence was the suppression of a potential feminist movement enacted in the post–World War II period by the series of the Communist Party's restructuring of the "Anti-fascist Front of Women" (*Antifašistički front žena*, or "AFŽ"), later called "The Women's Conference." The restructuring weakened this mass women's organization. The organization was also gradually pressed into dealing less with specifically women's problems and more with the ideological issues of a "new" society, and consequently lost its large membership. However, positive state policies regarding woman as a worker or major family care provider, to a significant extent, were also a product of the work (within the political system) of this—although gradually considerably weakened—"Women's Conference." See Lydia Sklevicky, "Emancipated Integration or Integrated Emancipation: The Case of Post-revolutionary Yugoslavia," in *Current Issues in Women's History*, ed. Angerman, Binnema, Keunen, Poels, and Zirkzee (London and New York: Routledge, 1989).

In other words, even though women were recognized as a specific group in their workplace and also as mothers and major family care providers, the fact that this differentiation was done by the state naturalized this recognition and corresponding policies. Also, neither state nor society (if one can make such gross generalizations about the "society" for a moment) explicitly recognized women as a specific group in their homes and their private lives. Vrkljan's writing about herself as a woman in her private and domestic life thus reacted to the absence of gender consciousness with regard to these very particular woman's subject positions.

5. Irena Vrkljan, *Svila, škare* (*Silk, Scissors*) (Zagreb, Croatia: Grafički zavod Hrvatske, 1984), epigraph; subsequently cited as *Silk*. Unless otherwise stated, quotations from Vrkljan's books other than *Marina* are translated by Gordana Crnković.

6. Defined within the Yugoslav cultural context of the time and allowing the wide differences among the country's respective republics and between urban and rural settings, the terms "individuals" and "individualism" convey meanings somewhat different from the ones developed in societies in which both the economic system and dominant cultural self-perception have been based on individualism, and where the terms might connote, for example, the negation of wider social self-perception and organized activity, or the apolitical nature of self-interested, bourgeois "individuals." Yugoslavia's history would not give the same social function and political potential to individualism. There, the economic basis (capitalism), ideology, discourse, and agency of individualism have always been more or less

absent, and what the country has had instead was the group-oriented discourse and agency of nation, family, peasantry, intelligentsia, the proletarian class, the party, and so on. Post–World War II socialism thus did not have to suppress individualism as much as it had to recast the already existing group-based identity formation.

The post–World War II period in Yugoslavia was characterized by the official (and, for some people, genuine) ideology of a "new socialist person," one whose self-perception revolved around relationships with other people, whose needs could be satisfied only by satisfying the needs of others, whose identity, at its deepest level, was the negation of the bourgeois "monad." The "individualism" was in many ways equated with selfishness, self-centeredness, or taking advantage of others. In this period, Yugoslavs found means to express themselves as workers, experts, journalists, managers, politicians, peasants, and so on, but rarely as particular individuals whose lives were not fully exhausted by being a model worker, a mother, a professional, or a supporter or an opponent of this or that political stance.

The absence of individualism—as the strong historical and social awareness of uniqueness of any particular person—led to the lack of articulation of those aspects of lives that cannot be expressed by the speech of a group. Unexpressed, unnamed, and unarticulated, the unique features of one's particular life or opinions have continually been creating shapes and problems that Yugoslavs have had difficulty addressing and acknowledging as legitimate because of this very lack of the conceptual apparatus and discourses of individualism.

7. *Silk, Scissors* was published in Zagreb in 1984, *Marina or About Biography* in 1986, *Berlin Manuscript* in 1988, and *Dora, This Autumn* in 1991.

In the 1980s, the quality of life in Yugoslavia declined from the relatively peaceful period of prosperity in the 1960s and 1970s to a condition in which over one thousand percent yearly inflation prevailed, the standard of living fell sharply, the unemployment rate grew, and national hostilities within the country began to escalate. The crisis of the 1980s was not only economic and political but also ideological, moral, and cultural.

The violence started in the summer of 1991 in Slovenia. One could, however, perhaps see the March of 1989 confrontation of JNA (*Jugoslavenska narodna armija,* Yugoslav People's Army) with Albanian civilians in Kosovo as the announcement of the approaching war.

8. One could note here that one of Dositej's favorite thinkers was a French philosopher Michel de Montaigne, who wrote that he considers all men his countrymen and respects a brave Pole as much as a Frenchman (*Essays*, trans. J. M. Cohen [Harmondsworth: Penguin, 1987], 3:9), and who condemned European colonialism in America with the words:

> What a compensation it would have been, and what an improvement to this whole earthly globe, if the first examples of our behavior offered to these peoples had caused them to admire and imitate our virtue, and had

established between them and us a brotherly intercourse and understanding! How easy it would have been to turn to good account minds so innocent and so eager to learn, which had, for the most part, made such good natural beginnings! On the contrary, we have taken advantage of their ignorance and inexperience to bend them more easily to treachery, lust, covetousness, and to every kind of inhumanity and cruelty, on the model and after the example of our own manners. Who ever valued the benefits of trade and commerce at so high a price? So many towns razed to the ground, so many nations exterminated, so many millions put to the sword, and the richest and fairest part of the world turned upside down for the benefit of the pearl and pepper trades! More commercial victories! Never did ambition, never did public hatreds drive men, one against another, to such terrible acts of hostility, and to such miserable disasters. (279)

9. Numerous books are written on Vuk Stefanović Karadžić in the former Yugoslavia, most of them unambiguously laudatory. My reading of Karadžić's effects is primarily informed by a critical account of Karadžić, written by one of the best Yugoslav writers, Bosnian Meša Selimović. Meša Selimović, *Za i protiv Vuka (For and Against Vuk)* (Sarajevo, Bosnia and Herzegovina: Svjetlost, 1970).

10. Autobiographies were not entirely absent in the nineteenth century either. One should only think of the thousand-page-long *Diary* by a Croatian woman, Dragojla Jarnević. However, even when present, autobiographies in the nineteenth century did not have the great prominence that Dositej's eighteenth-century work had had.

11. Though born in Belgrade, Irena Vrkljan is a Croatian author, and one can argue that it is not appropriate to discuss her work in relation to Serbian figures Obradović and Karadžić, given the largely separate Croatian and Serbian literary traditions. I am not claiming any factual or conscious literary relation on Vrkljan's part; Karadžić's work, however, was so immensely influential for the creation of modern Serbian culture that it filtered through, in this or that variant, to the culture of the former Yugoslavia in which Croatian and Serbian cultures influenced and interacted with each other (the former Yugoslavia was formed in 1918, was named "Yugoslavia" in 1929, and was dissolved in 1991). After World War II, the Socialist Federal Republic of Yugoslavia (*Socijalistička Federativna Republika Jugoslavia* was the full name of the country, succeeding the previous name of the Federal People's Republic of Yugoslavia, *Federativna Narodna Republika Jugoslavija*) built its cultural identity on an uneasy tension (more rejection than acceptance) toward discourses of individualism and on attempts to articulate and promote this people's identity and cultural policies, where the very concept of "people" was decisively—whether one knew it or not—influenced by Vuk Karadžić.

Vrkljan, who herself repeatedly mentions both her literary peers and her personal friends from the entire area of the former Yugoslavia, should not be seen only within her own national literary tradition, but also in relation to the major cultural tensions of both national and "Yugoslav" realms. With regard to these tensions, the line of division falls not on national borders but rather between writers like Croatian Vrkljan, Serbian Kiš, Bosnian Selimović, and others, on the one hand, who fought for the creation of critical individuality (and were thus spiritual heirs of Dositej Obradović) and against group-based and easily manipulated populist discourses and the other set of writers and "cultural workers," on the other hand, who promoted such populist discourses both in the period of the former Yugoslavia and that of its successor states. The influence of this other group can be seen as following the tradition of Vuk Karadžić's work and its rejection of individualism and intellectual or literary things that were not "spoken by the people."

12. As Celia Hawkesworth writes, in this work "[l]anguage is not an arbitrary means of providing form, but a vital instrument in the search for authenticity." And she continues, "It is necessary to know the story in order to begin to understand the meaning of the words. . . ." ("Irena Vrkljan: *Marina, or About Biography*," *The Slavonic and East European Review* 69, no. 2 [April 1991]: 222, 227).

13. Having grown up in a country in which some genuine socialists had waged a constant battle, in all aspects of society and culture, with those who took power in the name of socialism, Irena Vrkljan could hardly have been satisfied with the project of individualism, which fully abandons the visions and sometimes the realities of these "inspiring" socialists and which shapes itself as a self-centered self-absorption. "Elika's Soups," a narrative from *Silk, Scissors*, gives a portrayal of one of these "genuine" socialists. While I, an individual woman, want to be "I" apart from the group/dictionary-determined self-constitution, at the same time I want to be related to others, a part of "we" and relevant for us, although a differently functioning part of "we," which itself is different from that "we" commonly enforced upon me.

14. Hawkesworth, "Irena Vrkljan," 223.

15. Vrkljan's individualism of togetherness, while defying the closure of solipsistic individualism, is also radically different from anti-individualistic collectivism and group-based self-constitution, which was characteristic of the Yugoslav cultural context. "Bad" collectivism manifested itself as a uniform identity that was imposed on all, homogenized society, and in relation to which individualism as uniqueness or difference was an aberration. In contrast to this "bad" collectivism, Vrkljan's individualism as togetherness (or relational identity) created in *Marina* is based on the interactions and relations among individuals designed by the individuals themselves and not imposed on them by the outside center of power.

16. Howe herself uses the term, naming one of her chapters "Archaeology" (37).

17. Howe uses this phrase as the title of one of her chapters (75).

18. This excerpt also exemplifies an unrelated but very important point often mentioned with regard to Howe, namely that she is "more than any American writer I can think of except perhaps Melville or Henry Adams, burdened by history. . . ." Peter Quartermain, *Disjunctive Poetics: From Gertrude Stein and Louis Zukofsky to Susan Howe* (Cambridge: Cambridge University Press, 1992), 194.

19. Marina Tsvetaeva, *Povest o Sonječki* (*A Story About Sonechka*), trans. Aleksandar Badnjarević (Novi Sad, Yugoslavia: Bratstvo-Jedinstvo, 1986), 107.

20. "Myself was as another, now 'I' dare to go farther" (61). "Her talent was synthetic; she used other writers, grasped straws from the bewildering raveling of Being wherever and whenever she could use them. Crucial was her ability to spin straw into gold." (28)

21. Irena Vrkljan, *Berlinski rukopis* (*Berlin Manuscript*) (Zagreb, Croatia: Grafički zavod Hrvatske, 1988), 66.

Afterword

1. Erich Auerbach, *Mimesis: The Representation of Reality in Western Literature*, trans. Willard R. Trask (Princeton: Princeton University Press, 1974), 556.

2. This phrase comes from Christa Wolf's novel *The Quest for Christa T.*, 175.

Selected Bibliography

Auerbach, Erich. *Mimesis: The Representation of Reality in Western Literature*. Trans. Willard R. Trask. Princeton, N.J.: Princeton University Press, 1974.

Bakhtin, Mikhail Mikhailovich. *The Dialogic Imagination*. Trans. Caryl Emerson and Michael Holquist. Ed. Michael Holquist. Austin: University of Texas Press, 1981.

Baudrillard, Jean. *Selected Writings*. Ed. Mark Poster. Stanford, Calif.: Stanford University Press, 1988.

Benjamin, Walter. *Illuminations*. Trans. Harry Zohn. Ed. Hannah Arendt. New York: Schocken Books, 1969.

Berman, Russell A. *The Rise of the Modern German Novel*. Cambridge: Harvard University Press, 1986.

———. *Modern Culture and Critical Theory: Art, Politics, and the Legacy of the Frankfurt School*. Madison: University of Wisconsin Press, 1989.

Bloch, Ernst et al. *Aesthetics and Politics*. Trans. and ed. Ronald Taylor. London: NLB, 1977.

Borowski, Tadeusz. *This Way for the Gas, Ladies and Gentlemen*. Trans. Barbara Vedder. New York: Penguin Books, 1976.

———. *Pożegnanie z Marią; Kamienny świat*. 2d ed. Warsaw: Państwowy Instytut Wydawniczy, 1977.

Brodsky, Joseph. Introduction to *A Tomb for Boris Davidovich*, by Danilo Kiš. New York: Penguin Books, 1980.

Bross, Addison, trans. "Five Poems by Tadeusz Borowski." *The Polish Review* 28, no. 3 (1983): 43–49.

Brown, Norman O. "'John Cage': A Lecture." *Bucknell Review: A Scholarly Journal of Letters, Arts and Sciences* 32, no. 2 (1989): 97–118.

Cage, John. *Silence*. Middletown, Conn.: Wesleyan University Press, 1961; reprint, Middletown, Conn.: Wesleyan Paperback, 1973.

———. *Empty Words*. Middletown, Conn.: Wesleyan University Press, 1981.

———. *A Year from Monday*. Middletown, Conn.: Wesleyan University Press, 1985.

———. *I–VI*. Cambridge: Harvard University Press, 1990.

———. "Overpopulation and Art." In *John Cage: Composed in America*, ed. Marjorie Perloff and Charles Junkerman. Chicago: University of Chicago Press, 1994.

Crnković, Gordana P. "Why Should You Write about Eastern Europe, or: Why Should You Write about 'the Other'?" *Feminist Issues* 12, no. 2 (fall 1992): 21–42.

Doyle, Waddick. "Being an Other to Oneself: First Person Narration in Kazuo Ishiguro's *The Remains of the Day.*" In *L'Alterité dans la littérature et la culture du monde anglophone.* Le Mans, France: l'Université du Maine, 1993.

Drewnowski, Tadeusz. *Ucieczka z kamiennego świata (o Tadeuszu Borowskim) (Escape from the World of Stone* [*on Tadeusz Borowski*]). Warsaw: Państwowy Instytut Wydawniczy, 1962.

Eagleton, Terry. *The Ideology of the Aesthetic.* Oxford: Basil Blackwell, 1990.

Fiumara, Gemma Corradi. *The Other Side of Language: A Philosophy of Listening.* London and New York: Routledge, 1990.

Frye, Northrop. *The Anatomy of Criticism.* Princeton, N.J.: Princeton University Press, 1957.

Fukuyama, Francis. *The End of History and the Last Man.* New York: Avon Books, 1993.

Gauss, Karl-Markus. "Na dnu Panonskog mora: Danilo Kiš" ("On the Bottom of the Panonian Sea: Danilo Kiš"). In *Uništenje Srednje Evrope (The Destruction of Central Europe)*, trans. Truda Stamać. Zagreb, Croatia: Durieux, 1994.

Gombrowicz, Witold. *Diary.* Vol. 1. Trans. Lillian Vallee. Evanston: Northwestern University Press, 1988.

Gorjup, Branko. "Danilo Kiš: From 'Enchantment' to 'Documentation.'" *Canadian Slavonic Papers* 29, no. 4 (December 1987): 387–94.

————. "Textualizing the Past: The Function of Memory and History in Kiš's Fiction." *The Review of Contemporary Fiction* 14, no. 1 (spring 1994): 161–68.

Grassi, Ernesto. *Moć mašte (The Power of Imagination).* Trans. Maja Hausler. Zagreb, Croatia: Školska knjiga, 1981.

Haraszti, Miklós. *The Velvet Prison.* Trans. Katalim Stephen Landesmann, with the assistance of Steve Wasserman. New York: A New Republic Book, 1987.

Havel, Václav. *Václav Havel or Living in Truth.* Ed. Jan Vladislav. London: Faber and Faber, 1986.

Hawkesworth, Celia. "Irena Vrkljan: *Marina, or About Biography.*" *The Slavonic and East European Review* 69, no. 2 (April 1991): 221–31.

————. "*Silk, Scissors, Garden, Ashes:* The Autobiographical Writings of Irena Vrkljan and Danilo Kiš." In *Literature and Politics in Eastern Europe: Selected Papers from the Fourth World Congress for Soviet and East European Studies, Harrogate, 1990.* New York: St. Martin's Press, 1992.

Hegel, Georg Wilhelm Friedrich. *The Philosophy of Right.* Trans. T. M. Knox. Oxford: Clarendon Press, 1965.

————. *Phenomenology of Spirit.* Trans. A. V. Miller. Oxford: Clarendon Press, 1977.

————. *Aesthetics: Lectures on Fine Art.* Trans. T. M. Knox. Oxford: Clarendon Press, 1975.

Heidegger, Martin. "The Origin of the Work of Art." In *Poetry, Language, Thought*, trans. Albert Hofstadter. New York: Harper and Row, 1975.

Horvath, Brooke. "Danilo Kiš: An Introduction." *The Review of Contemporary Fiction* 14, no. 1 (spring 1994): 97–106.

Howe, Susan. *My Emily Dickinson*. Berkeley, Calif.: North Atlantic Books, 1985.

Ishiguro, Kazuo. *A Pale View of Hills*. New York: Putnam, 1982; reprint, New York: Vintage Books, 1990.

———. *An Artist of the Floating World*. New York: Putnam, 1986; reprint, New York: Vintage Books, 1989.

———. "An Interview with Kazuo Ishiguro." By Gregory Mason. *Contemporary Literature* 30, no. 3 (fall 1989):335–47.

———. *The Remains of the Day*. London: Faber and Faber, 1989; New York: Alfred A. Knopf, 1989; reprint, New York: Vintage Books, 1990.

———. "An Interview with Kazuo Ishiguro." By Christopher Bigsby. *European English Messenger* (fall 1990): 26–29.

———. "Stuck on the Margins: An Interview with Kazuo Ishiguro." By Allan Vorda. In *Face to Face: Interviews with Contemporary Novelists*. Houston, Tex.: Rice University Press, 1993.

Ishiguro, Kazuo, and Oe Kenzaburo. "The Novelist in Today's World: A Conversation." *boundary 2: An International Journal of Literature and Culture* 18, no. 3 (fall 1991): 109–22.

Jablan, Radovan. "Danilo Kiš izbliza" ("Danilo Kiš from a Close Distance"). *Stvaranje: Časopis za književnost i kulturu* 45, no. 10 (October 1990): 1083–91.

Jameson, Frederic. *The Political Unconscious: Narrative as a Socially Symbolic Act*. Ithaca, New York: Cornell University Press, 1981.

———. *Late Marxism*. London and New York: Verso, 1990.

Kesić, Vesna. "Slovenski dan poslije" ("Slovenian Day After"). *Danas* 496 (August 20, 1991): 53.

King, Bruce. "The New Internationalism: Shiva Naipaul, Salman Rushdie, Buchi Emecheta, Timothy Mo and Kazuo Ishiguro." In *The British and Irish Novel Since 1960*, ed. James Acheson. New York: St. Martin's Press, 1991.

Kiš, Danilo. *Čas anatomije (The Anatomy Lesson)*. Belgrade, Yugoslavia: Nolit, 1978.

———. *A Tomb for Boris Davidovich*. Trans. Duška Mikić-Mitchell. New York: Penguin Books, 1980.

———. "Entretien avec Danilo Kiš." Interview by Norbert Czarny. *La Quinzaine Littéraire* 447 (September 16–30, 1985): 17.

———. *Garden, Ashes*. Trans. William J. Hannaher. London: Faber and Faber, 1985.

———. "Tražim mesto pod suncem za sumnju" ("I Am Looking for a Place under the Sun to Put Doubt"). *Izraz* 68, no. 9 (September 1990):195–208.

———. *The Encyclopedia of the Dead*. Trans. Michael Henry Heim. New York: Penguin Books, 1991.

————. "Autobiographical Sketch (Short Autobiography)." *The Review of Contemporary Fiction* 14, no. 1 (spring 1994): 117–18.

Klaić, Dragan. "Danilo Kiš: The Theatrical Connection." *The Review of Contemporary Fiction* 14, no. 1 (spring 1994): 202–7.

Kostelanetz, Richard. *Conversing with Cage.* New York: Limelight Editions, 1991.

Kott, Jan. Introduction to *This Way for the Gas, Ladies and Gentlemen,* by Tadeusz Borowski. New York: Penguin Books, 1976.

Krivokapić, Boro, ed. *Treba li spaliti Kiša? (Should Kiš Be Burned?).* Zagreb, Croatia: Globus, 1980.

Kuhiwczak, Piotr. "Beyond Self: A Lesson from the Concentration Camps." *Canadian Review of Comparative Literature/Revue Canadienne de Littérature Comparée* 19, no. 3 (September 1992): 395–405.

Kundera, Milan. *Testaments Betrayed.* Trans. Linda Asher. New York: HarperCollins, 1995.

Laclau, Ernesto and Chantal Mouffe. *Hegemony and Socialist Strategy.* New York: Verso, 1985.

Longinović, Tomislav Z. *Borderline Culture: The Politics of Identity in Four Twentieth-Century Slavic Novels.* Fayetteville: University of Arkansas Press, 1993.

Lukács, Georg. *The Theory of the Novel.* Cambridge: MIT Press, 1989.

Marx, Karl. *The Marx-Engels Reader.* 2d ed. Ed. Robert C. Tucker. New York and London: W. W. Norton, 1978.

Mason, Gregory. "Inspiring Images: The Influence of the Japanese Cinema on the Writings of Kazuo Ishiguro." *East-West Film Journal* 3, no. 2 (June 1989): 39–52.

Matillon, Janine. "Entretien avec Danilo Kiš: Qu'est-ce qu'un écrivain yougoslave à Paris?" *La Quinzaine Littéraire* 317 (January 1980): 17.

Mihailovich, Vasa D. "Faction or Fiction in *A Tomb for Boris Davidovich:* The Literary Affair." *The Review of Contemporary Fiction* 14, no. 1 (spring 1994): 169–73.

Montaigne, Michel de. *Essays.* Vol. 3. Trans. J. M. Cohen. Harmondsworth: Penguin, 1987.

Morson, Gary Saul, and Caryl Emerson. *Mikhail Bakhtin: Creation of a Prosaics.* Stanford, Calif.: Stanford University Press, 1990.

Patey, Caroline. "When Ishiguro Visits the West Country: An Essay on *The Remains of the Day.*" *Acme: Annali della Facolta di Lettere e Filosofia dell'Universita degli Studi di Milano* 44, no. 2 (May–August 1991): 135–55.

Perloff, Marjorie. "The Portrait of the Artist as Collage-Text: Pound's Gaudier-Brzeska and the 'Italic' Texts of John Cage." *The American Poetry Review* 11, no. 3 (May–June 1982): 19–29.

————. "Non-obstruction et interpenetration: La Poétique de John Cage." Trans. Susan Santolini and Daniel Charles. *Revue d'Esthétique* 13–15 (1987–88): 381–92.

————. "'Collision or Collusion with History': The Narrative Lyric of Susan Howe." *Contemporary Literature* 30, no. 4 (1989): 518–34.

Pratt, Mary Louise. "Scratches on the Face of the Country; or, What Mr. Barrow Saw in the Land of the Bushmen." In *"Race," Writing and Difference,* ed. Henry Louis Gates, Jr. Chicago: University of Chicago Press, 1986.

Quartermain, Peter. *Disjunctive Poetics: From Gertrude Stein and Louis Zukofsky to Susan Howe.* Cambridge: Cambridge University Press, 1992.

Romanowicz, Zofia. *Passage through the Red Sea.* Trans. Virgilia Peterson. New York: Harcourt, Brace and World, 1962.

Salivarová, Zdena. *Summer in Prague.* Trans. Marie Winn. New York: Harper and Row, 1973.

Selimović, Meša. *Za i protiv Vuka.* (*For and Against Vuk*). Sarajevo, Bosnia and Herzegovina: Svjetlost, 1970.

Shishkoff, Serge. "Košava in a Coffee Pot, or a Dissection of a Literary *cause célèbre.*" *Cross Currents* 6 (1987): 341–71.

Sklevicky, Lydia. "Emancipated Integration or Integrated Emancipation: The Case of Post-revolutionary Yugoslavia." In *Current Issues in Women's History,* ed. Angerman, Binnema, Keunen, Poels, and Zirkzee. London and New York: Routledge, 1989.

Solar, Milivoj. *Mit o avangardi i mit o dekadenciji (Myth of the Avant-garde and Myth of Decadence).* Belgrade, Yugoslavia: Nolit, 1986.

Stavans, Ilan."Danilo Kiš in Buenos Aires." *The Review of Contemporary Fiction* 14, no. 1 (spring 1994): 174–79.

Swift, Graham. "Kazuo Ishiguro." *BOMB* 29 (fall 1989): 22–23.

Szpakowska, Małgorzata. "Kamienny świat pod kamiennym niebem." *Teksty: Teoria Literatury; Krytyka; Interpretacja* 2, no. 4 (1973): 139–45.

Tsvetaeva, Marina. *Povest o Sonječki (A Story About Sonechka).* Trans. Aleksandar Badnjarević. Novi Sad, Yugoslavia: Bratstvo-Jedinstvo, 1986.

Volarić, Svetlana. *U paklu su zvijezde ravnodušno sjale (Stars Shone Indifferently in the Hell).* Belgrade, Yugoslavia: Prosveta, 1966.

Vrkljan, Irena. *Svila, škare (Silk, Scissors).* Zagreb, Croatia: Grafički zavod Hrvatske, 1984.

————. *Marina ili o biografiji.* 2d ed. Zagreb, Croatia: Grafički zavod Hrvatske, 1987.

————. *Berlinski rukopis (Berlin Manuscript).* Zagreb, Croatia: Grafički zavod Hrvatske, 1988.

————. *Marina or About Biography.* Trans. Celia Hawkesworth. Zagreb, Croatia: Durieux/The Bridge, 1991.

Wain, Peter. "The Historical-Political Aspect of the Novels of Kazuo Ishiguro." *Language and Culture* (Hokkaido, Japan) 23 (1992): 177–205.

Walc, Jan. "'When the Earth Is No Longer a Dream and Cannot Be Dreamed through to the End.'" *The Polish Review* 32, no. 2 (1987): 181–94.

Wall, Kathleen. "*The Remains of the Day* and Its Challenges to Theories of Unreliable Narration." *Journal of Narrative Technique* (*JNT*) 24, no. 1 (1994): 18–42.

White, Hayden. "The Value of Narrativity in the Representation of Reality." In *On Narrative*, ed. W. J. T. Mitchell. Chicago: University of Chicago Press, 1981.

Wiesel, Elie. *The Night Trilogy*. Trans. Stella Rodway. New York: Farrar, Straus and Giroux, 1987.

Wirth, Andrzej. "A Discovery of Tragedy (The Incomplete Account of Tadeusz Borowski)." *The Polish Review* 12, no. 3 (1967): 43–52.

Wolf, Christa. *The Quest for Christa T.* Trans. Christopher Middleton. New York: Farrar, Straus and Giroux, 1979.

———. *Cassandra*. Trans. Jan van Heurck. New York: Farrar, Straus and Giroux, 1988.

Yoshioka, Fumio. "Beyond the Division of East and West: Kazuo Ishiguro's *A Pale View of Hills*." *Studies in English Literature* 101 (1988): 71–86.

Žižek, Slavoj. "Slovenski dan poslije" ("Slovenian Day After"). Interview by Kesić Vesna. *Danas* 496 (August 20, 1991): 53.

Index

Theory over literary criticism and literature, 8–10

This Way for the Gas, Ladies and Gentlemen, 2, 12, 63–91. *See also* "Auschwitz, Our Home (A Letter)"; Borowski, Tadeusz; "Day at Harmenz, A"; "World of Stone, The"
  The Remains of the Day versus, 88, 90
  theme of, 66
  time of writing of, 136–37 n. 3

Tomb for Boris Davidovich, A, 2, 12, 15–61. *See also* Kiš, Danilo
  anticlosure practices of absurdity in, 40–44
  chronicle versus history in, 33
  closure of absolute irony and, 30–31
  comparison to Wolf's *Cassandra* of, 132 n. 18
  excerpts from, 21, 22, 23, 26, 32, 33, 35, 37, 39, 40, 41
  Hegelian triad of, 37–40
  as metaphor of the "empty tomb" and absence of history, 21–23
  missing synthesis in, 39–40
  myth of revolution example in, 35–36
  negativity of antithesis in, 38–39
  as reclaimed referentiality, 31
  Silence and, 21
  texts that interpret the world in, 37–38

Tsvetaeva, Marina, 150 n. 19

Vertical construction of language, 44–46, 47, 48, 52, 57, 58, 59

Vrkljan, Irena, 2, 12, 13, 93–123. See also *Marina or About Biography*; *Silk, Scissors*
  on autobiographical writings of, 95, 145–46 n. 4
  biographical sketch of, 95

biographies of words in work of, 100–7, 110
cross-cultural identity in writing of, 106–7
feminist tone of writings of, 95, 100, 145–46 n. 4
individualism and absence of politics in works of, 96–97, 146–47 n. 6, 149 n. 15
individualism by, 149 n. 13
Karadžić and, 148–49 n. 11
language and gender problems presented by, 130 n. 12
literature against closure of gender and, 93–123
Obradović and, 100
poetry as art of social relations and, 122–23
relational emphatic identity in *Dora, This Autumn,* 121
relational feminine identity in writing of, 119–22
relational subjectivity in writing of, 112, 113–14
Silk, Scissors and autobiography of a woman by, 95–107
writing as reading by, 105–6

Walc, Jan, 136 n. 1
White, Hayden, 135 nn. 49–50
Wolf, Christa, 132 nn. 18, 20, 133 n. 31, 150 n. 2
Women's relational identity, 111–12, 119–22
"World of Stone, The," 80–84
  and announcement of the "immortal epic," 80–84
  excerpts from, 81, 82–83
Writing as reading, 105–6

Žižek, Slavoj, 134 n. 40